Economic Development Programs for Cities, Counties and Towns

ECONOMIC DEVELOPMENT PROGRAMS FOR CITIES, COUNTIES AND TOWNS
SECOND EDITION

JOHN M. LEVY _____

New York
Westport, Connecticut
London

Copyright Acknowledgments

Tables 6.1 through 6.5 are taken from the author's article "What Local Economic Developers Actually Do: Location Quotients versus Press Releases," reprinted by permission of the *Journal of the American Planning Association*, Vol. 56, No. 2 (Spring 1990).

Library of Congress Cataloging-in-Publication Data

Levy, John M.
    Economic development programs for cities, counties and towns /
John M. Levy. — 2nd ed.
      p.   cm.
    Includes bibliographical references.
    ISBN 0-275-93366-0 (alk. paper). — ISBN 0-275-93760-7
(pbk. : alk. paper)
    1. Urban policy—United States. 2. Community development, Urban—
United States. 3. Federal aid to community development—United
States. I. Title.
HT123.L39   1990
338.973—dc20   90-32301

Library of Congress Catalog Card Number: 90-32301
ISBN: 0-275-93366-0 (hb.)
     0-275-93760-7 (pbk.)

First published in 1990

Praeger Publishers, One Madison Avenue, New York, NY 10010
An imprint of Greenwood Publishing Group, Inc.

Printed in the United States of America

∞™

The paper used in this book complies with the Permanent
Paper Standard issued by the National Information Standards
Organization (Z39.48-1984).

10 9 8 7 6 5 4 3 2 1

To Lucie, Rachel, Bernie, and Kara

Contents

Tables

Preface

The reader who is familiar with the first edition of this work will note that this edition contains new material and that much material from the first edition has been deleted. Chapter 4, "Recent Economic Changes," focuses on deindustrialization and a number of foreign-trade-related matters. For an increasing number of firms and communities the prime competitor is not located in the next county or the next state but across the ocean. Thus the economic developer needs a global perspective. State governments, partly because of increasing international competition, are becoming more important players in the game. Thus this edition adds Chapter 5, "The Role of the States." Chapter 6, "What Does and Does Not Work," also is new. It is based largely on the author's survey of economic development practitioners in the spring of 1989. To the author's knowledge it is the most recent and complete description of practitioner experience available.

Another addition to this work is the inclusion of a simple, generic PC-based fiscal impact model and a few words about PC-based databases. When the first edition was written, the PC was just making its appearance, and in most cases the use of a computer for fiscal impact analysis implied retaining a consultant. This is no longer the case. The cost of relatively friendly software for developing databases has become almost negligible, and there are numerous people, particularly people newly educated, who are quite competent to develop and maintain an in-house, instantly accessible database.

Intermunicipal economic competition is increasing, and the number of communities mounting economic development programs continues to grow. In many cases the potential results of a community economic development program are oversold. Chapter 7, "Reasonable Expectations," provides a basis for estimating the likely benefits and results of embarking upon an economic development program.

Chapter 13, "Local Economic Development in the National Picture," is new. In recent years there has been considerable discussion of the aggregate effects of local economic development activity. This chapter is an attempt to lay out some of the major arguments within a framework of traditional neo-classical economic theory.

One major change in the 1980s has been the withdrawal of the federal government from the local economic development scene. This change accounts for most of the deletions from the first edition. That edition included rather detailed accounts of the Economic Development Administration (EDA) and the Urban Development Action Grant (UDAG) program. EDA is now operating with less than one-fourth the real dollars it had at the beginning of the decade, and the UDAG program is effectively over. In this edition, these programs are mentioned only in passing. The first edition contained an extended discussion of Industrial Revenue Bond (IRB) financing. In 1981, when the first edition appeared, IRBs were the most widely used financial incentive available to the local economic developer. But by the end of 1989 they were restricted to a very small range of activities and their inclusion would hardly be justified in this edition. They, too, are mentioned only in passing.

The first edition contained an extended discussion of the Comprehensive Employment and Training Act (CETA). At its peak, CETA delivered over $8 billion a year in federal manpower funds. But CETA was terminated in 1983 and replaced with the Jobs Training Partnership Act (JTPA), which, in real terms, is funded at no more than one-fourth the level of CETA. JTPA is discussed in Chapter 11, but in substantially less detail than was CETA in the previous edition. Following the discussion of CETA, the first edition devoted a chapter to manpower planning. That chapter has been dropped from this edition. It is an arguable choice, but the writer's view is that very little manpower planning is associated with local economic development efforts today. This is both his direct impression and the finding of the survey noted earlier. While it may well be that manpower planning should be an integral part of the local economic development scene, it does not seem to be so. The author's intent is to describe the field as it is.

Finally, the reader should be aware that this book parts company with much of the academic literature on local economic development over a key issue: It treats local economic development as primarily a sales and political activity whose integration into a systematic community planning process is, unfortunately, often minimal. That view is far from universal. In fact, judging from books on the subject, it is probably a minority view. There are some fine books that approach the subject from a very different perspective and present economic development as part of a systematic community planning process with the sales and promotional functions being at the end of the process, rather than at the center, as they are in this volume. Several such books are mentioned in the early chapters of this book.

Economic Development Programs for Cities, Counties and Towns

Introduction

There are estimated to be between 15,000 and 18,000 organizations in the United States devoted to the promotion of local economic growth. They appear in a bewildering variety of forms—among others, governmental and quasi-governmental agencies, nonprofit corporations, and local development corporations. They range in size from chambers of commerce, with minimal budgets and no paid staff, to development corporations with large staffs and multimillion-dollar budgets.

How much the nation spends on local economic development is not known because funds come from so many sources and because the government contribution comes from both sides of the budget—direct expenditures and tax expenditures.[1] A very conservative estimate would place the total expenditures at over $10 billion. The actual total may be several times that. A survey taken by the author showed an average agency staff size of 6.2 people, not including the director. If we assume, rather cautiously, an average staff size (including director) of five, a total of 15,000 agencies, and an average wage of $25,000, then the wage bill alone is almost $2 billion. If we add an overhead factor of 100 percent for fringes, rent, travel, advertising, printing, and so on, we have an agency operating cost in the $4 billion vicinity.

Direct federal expenditures for local economic development in the late 1980s probably add another $4 billion or more. The estimated loss of tax revenues on Industrial Revenue Bonds (IRBs) was about $2.8 billion.[2] Direct grant programs like those of the Economic Development Administration and HUD's Community Development Block Grant (CDBG) also provide funds used for economic development purposes.

At the local level, apart from the agency operating costs noted above, there are direct expenditures on items such as community industrial parks and shell buildings. There are also property tax and, occasionally, sales tax abatements. The states offer a large array of tax expenditures, such as investment tax credits, sales tax abatements, and concessions on corporate income rate writedowns and loan and mortgage guarantees.

Local economic development is an intensely competitive activity. Whether the development agency is striving to bring in a firm or to encourage an expansion, it is in competition with a very large number of rivals. Whether it is the competition to attract firms or the competition between communities for a limited amount of development funding, the economic developer exists in a world just as competitive as that of the firms which are his quarry—and sometimes more so.

If economic development is a goal so earnestly pursued by so many communities, it may seem odd for a book on economic development to begin with the question "Is a development program needed?" Nevertheless, it is a question that any community considering a program should ponder and a logical point at which to begin a book on economic development. Economic development offers many benefits to communities. Inevitably, it will exact some price. There are many valid and praiseworthy reasons for pursuing an active development policy. But there are also many not-so-praiseworthy reasons for doing so.

ECONOMIC DEVELOPMENT AND UNEMPLOYMENT

Perhaps the most common, and certainly the most readily justified, reason for a local economic development program is the need to create jobs both to reduce unemployment and to exert upward pressure on wages. The progenitor of modern local economic development programs originated in Mississippi during the Great Depression.[3] Named BAWI (Balance Agriculture with Industry), its goal was to provide manufacturing jobs for a desperately poor and often unemployed rural and small-town population. In recent years the two federal agencies most heavily involved in providing direct financial assistance to promote local economic development have made poverty and unemployment the primary criteria for funding eligibility.[4]

The justification for local economic development as a cure for unemployment and poverty rests upon one central fact: people are less mobile than capital. Were people as mobile as capital, the loss of an industry would be followed by an outmigration of workers and their dependents, preventing the unemployment rate from rising and the wage rate from falling. Conversely, the opening of a new industry would draw in enough new workers to prevent the unemployment rate from falling and wage rates from rising. In terms of labor markets, it would not be possible to justify local economic development programs.

But perfect mobility is not the case. The population adjusts only slowly to economic change. Nationally, the shift from coal to oil occurred in the 1940s, yet the population that had built up in parts of Kentucky, Ohio, West Virginia, and other eastern coal areas has largely remained in place to the present time, with persisting low wage levels and high unemployment rates. If at some time petroleum prices were to rise very sharply, the increased demand for coal might reverse the economic fortunes of some of these areas. If so, it would be a matter of jobs coming to people and not the reverse.

A similar immobility of labor in the face of job shifts is seen in urban areas. From 1969 through 1975, New York lost an incredible total of half a million jobs. Yet city population shrank only slightly. The job loss manifested itself more in increased unemployment, decreased labor-force participation, and increased public assistance than it did in outmigration of population. Since 1980 the city has gained back several hundred thousand jobs, but the total population has remained essentially stable.

When population does decline as a result of job losses, the decline is not generally an across-the-board one. Numerous studies show that those most prone to leave an economically declining area are younger adults with above-average incomes and above-average educations. To a lesser degree, there is a loss of children in the population because it is young adults who have young children. Age, poverty, and lack of education are all predispositions to immobility. This is hardly surprising, for it seems only reasonable that youth, education, and money should give people the energy and confidence to pull up stakes and move. Thus, declining areas often lose precisely the people they can least afford to lose. Let us consider some major indications that the local job market may be inadequate for the population it serves.

High Unemployment and Low Labor-Force Participation Rates

The unemployment rate is probably the most widely cited economic statistic in the United States. Obviously, persistently high rates are an indication of a mismatch between economic base and population, and are the single strongest reason for implementing a development program.

Persistent unemployment causes people to drop out of the labor force. The prospects for finding work may become so dim that potential workers simply stop looking. At that point they cease to be counted as unemployed. Thus, as useful as the unemployment rate may be, it does not present a full picture of the labor market. Low participation rates are an indication of the presence of discouraged workers and a signal that labor-market conditions may well be worse than the unemployment rate indicates. Participation rates by age, sex, and race provide an insight into labor-market conditions that the unemployment rate alone does not give. These insights may be useful in program design.

For example, a normal male participation rate, combined with a very low female participation rate, might suggest a development program targeted at bringing in or developing light-assembly or office activities that would be expected to provide a high percentage of jobs for women. A higher-than-average labor-force participation rate for women, accompanied by a lower-than-average rate for men, might suggest an economy that provides an adequate number of service, clerical, and domestic jobs but is in need of more blue-collar and industrial opportunities. (In fact, the higher-than-average female participation/lower-than-average male participation rate that often characterizes urban black populations results partly from the fact that clerical and domestic employment is more readily available for women than is manufacturing and other blue-collar employment for men.)

Cyclical Instability

Unemployment-rate fluctuations above the national average are an indication that an area is specialized in characteristically unstable industries. Typically, capital-goods and durable-goods manufacturing shows large cyclical changes. Industries heavily dependent upon federal procurement also may show large swings, though these will follow changes in the federal budget rather than the business cycle. A history of cyclical instability may argue for an economic development program that emphasizes diversification or that seeks to bring in industries noted for relative constancy of demand (much nondurable-goods manufacturing falls in this category, as do many service activities).

Low Levels of Personal or Family Income

Average wages may be low because an area has more than its share of low-wage industries, or because its industries pay lower wages than do their counterparts in other labor markets. The symptoms thus may be similar while the diseases are quite different. Family incomes may be low because of low wage rates or low participation rates. Two industrial areas that pay similar wages to male workers may exhibit very different family-income statistics if one offers numerous jobs for women while the other does not. To the extent that the problem is understood, a development program can be designed to deal with it.

A development program that brings jobs into an area—whether by attracting new firms or by encouraging present firms to expand—offers the prospect of tightening the labor market, with the effect of driving down the unemployment rate, pushing up participation rates, and elevating wages as the competition among firms for workers increases. Ideally, the program should be targeted at bringing in the types of jobs most needed. However, even if a program's retention and recruitment activities cannot be given a precise target—as is very often the case—almost any increase in jobs will have some tightening effects.

But here a caveat is important: People are much more mobile in the face of job opportunities than in the face of job losses. If a factory in a small town closes and 100 jobs are lost, the number of residents who move out may be extremely small. The job loss will manifest itself through some increase in unemployment and some decrease in participation rates. Some people who were dual jobholders may become single jobholders. On the other hand, should a new factory open in a comparable small town, a very considerable number of people may come in to take the new jobs. The decrease in unemployment and the increase in participation rates among the original population may thus be far smaller than a naive estimate would have indicated. This point is discussed in more detail in Chapter 12.

Writing about labor markets in southern towns that had gained industrial employment at a rapid pace, one writer noted:

Relocating manufacturers contend that they do not have to depend on workers already in town. They simply announce in, say, the Baltimore newspapers that they are headed for, say, Lynchburg, and the native sons return with Northern-acquired skills. In almost any Southern town from which blue-collar workers have migrated, some reluctantly, many have tired of the big city and would like to return, but they need a good job. When a new plant comes in, they come back. In fact, the hard corollary to this easy mobility is that local growth does not really lick the unemployment problem—all it does, in the long run, is enlarge the local labor force. Since it is the returning skilled workers who win away most of the new jobs, the town just gets bigger, still struggling with its chronic unemployment problem—its "unemployables."[5]

It is hardly surprising that the gaining of jobs is far more likely to encourage inmigration than the loss of jobs is likely to encourage immediate outmigration. It takes far less courage to move to a new job than it does to move into a new area with no guarantee of employment.

ECONOMIC DEVELOPMENT AND PROPERTY TAXES

In recent years, what might be regarded as a somewhat less legitimate reason for mounting economic development programs has come to the fore: property tax relief. Increasing costs of local government and increasing citizen resistance to rising local taxes—particularly the property tax—have put many local governments in an uncomfortable fiscal position. The passage of Proposition 13 in California, Proposition 2-½ in Massachusetts, and a number of other tax limitation initiatives at the end of the 1970s were clear testimony to the strength of citizen feeling. In some cases, the difficulty is compounded by constitutional limits on either bonded indebtedness or on the tax rate as a percentage of the value of taxable real property. For the community in a fiscal bind, whatever the cause, bringing in new commercial ratables that promise to yield far more in revenues than they will demand in services is an obvious solution to the problem.

The emphasis on economic development as a property tax relief program, rather than as a jobs program, is particularly common where the community is small relative to its labor market. Consider, for example, a small town in a metropolitan area. It can do little to affect its own labor market. Most of its residents do not work in that community, and most workers in that community are not residents. However, if a new commercial facility can be brought in, all of the property taxes it pays accrue to the treasury of that municipality. Thus in many suburban areas, there is intense competition among relatively prosperous communities motivated almost entirely by fiscal rather than labor-market considerations. The success of a development program is judged far more on the basis of the taxable value of new facilities than on the number of jobs they offer. In fact, the provision of jobs may be regarded only as an unpleasant side effect that must be accepted in order to get the ratable.

The fact that many communities pursue economic development even when there is no demonstrable labor-market need is clear in this response to a survey conducted by the writer. The response comes from a large suburban county in the northeastern United States that maintains a development staff of more than a dozen people.

[The] focus in _____ has been changed from finding jobs for people to finding people for jobs. Our unemployment rate is so low that it is actually a detriment. _____ has a definite shortage in affordable housing which makes the younger workforce move out of the county and work elsewhere.

What public purpose, other than pushing down property tax rates, can be served by a program that promotes job growth in an area of low unemployment and housing shortages?

OTHER MOTIVATIONS FOR LOCAL ECONOMIC DEVELOPMENT PROGRAMS

Another motivation behind many local economic development programs is that growth is good for the existing business community. Growth increases the demand for goods, services, and property. It thus benefits merchants, owners of service businesses, and owners of both vacant land and commercial and residential buildings.

Because economic development appears to offer something for so many diverse elements in the community—jobs for unemployed workers, increased sales for retailers, capital gains for property owners, increased loan business for local banks, higher rents for apartment owners, increased commissions for the local real estate brokerage industry—the economic developer often puts together a constituency of rather diverse elements. Union leaders and businessmen, wealthy property owners, and minority advocates, if able to agree on little else, can agree on the need for economic growth. Like politics, economic development makes strange bedfellows.

THE SIDE EFFECTS OF ECONOMIC DEVELOPMENT

If economic development programs offer improved labor-market conditions (from the workers' viewpoint), property-tax relief, and higher profits for many segments of the business community, are there cases in which public encouragement of economic growth is inadvisable?

A successful economic growth program will, inevitably, have side effects. Whether these are serious enough to argue against beginning a program is a matter to be determined case by case. But it is important to recognize these effects and anticipate them, rather than to discover them later.

Housing-Market Effects

Much of the demand for housing comes from the availability of jobs. Economic growth tightens housing markets. Prices and rents go up and vacancy rates go down. How much the market is tightened by economic growth will depend on many factors. One, obviously, is the amount of growth relative to the size of the housing market in which new workers must find shelter. Another, perhaps slightly less obvious, factor is the elasticity of the housing stock. Can the housing stock expand readily? Or are there physical or legal factors that constrain its expansion? Economic growth in San Francisco, where there is almost no unbuilt land remaining in the city, has produced extremely high housing prices—so high that the city has become an almost impossible market for many, if not most, single-income families with children.

In Fairfield County, Connecticut, a combination of rapid employment growth and much slower housing stock growth, in part the effect of strict land-use controls on the residential side, has produced very tight markets. As a result, the average selling price of a house in many communities may be several hundred thousand dollars. A comparable squeeze can be seen in a number of Washington, D.C., suburbs.

For the worker who benefits directly from economic growth, or for the family that is converted from a one- to a two-income family because of new employment opportunities, the higher housing costs may be a minor price to pay for newfound prosperity. For the property owner, the higher level of prices may be a much appreciated windfall. But for the retired person, or for anyone who is not a beneficiary of the tightened labor market, the higher price and rent levels may be a considerable burden. Wilbur Thompson notes: "It is irresponsible to promote local industrial expansion without coupling this action to a low income housing policy that picks up the pieces. But we do it all the time."[6] While that is a far stronger and more categorical statement than this writer would care to make, the fact is that there is a nexus between housing markets and job markets that ought to be thought about before embarking on a development program.

Environmental Effects

Environmental effects are more generally recognized than housing-market effects. All economic development has some environmental impact. For most activities other than power generation, materials processing, and some heavy industry, the most serious environmental effect is likely to stem from automotive emissions. Nonetheless, the effect is there and a community price must be paid. Often, the economic developer will find himself or herself at odds with local environmental movements. More will be said about this later, but he or she is often well advised to bring the environmental movement into the development-planning process early, rather than confronting it later in the media or the courts.

Land-Use Planning

Economic development programs can be the enemy of good land-use planning. When there is a strong push for new industry and when an agency feels great pressure to show results, there is a tendency for the community's long-term interest in good planning to take a back seat. If the developer lets the agency know that there are many other communities that will be happy to accommodate him or her if he or she cannot get the rezoning sought, the agency may well become the developer's advocate regardless of the long-term interest of the community. In fact, the economic developer may begin thinking of the planners as natural enemies, in spite of the fact that they are, in principle, both being paid to serve the interests of the same public. The planners, of course, may come to similar conclusions about the economic developer.

The situation becomes worse when the economic development is to take place in one community and the effects on land use or other planning concerns will be felt in an adjacent community. The populace of the adjacent community has no effective voice in the political processes of the community doing the development. Thus it has little ability to represent its own interest. The city or town central business district that has been devastated by a mall built just on the other side of the municipal line is probably the most common example of destructive interarea economic competition. The writer has no solution to the problem. Unfortunately, beggar-my-neighbor practices are often part of the game.

Social Stress, and Political and Fiscal Change

In general, economic growth promotes inmigration. Demographic change—in terms of both structure of population and size of population—will place some stress on the existing social fabric. The effects of inmigration may produce changes that are ultimately seen by most as beneficial, or inmigration resulting from development may prove traumatic, with massive increases in crime, alcoholism, prostitution. Again, it is hard to generalize. The opening of a think tank in suburbia and the initiation of a massive construction project in a small, isolated town both qualify as economic development, but they have little else in common.

To the extent that the incoming population is different from the in-place population in habits, values, and attitudes, economic growth promotes political change. This is not to say that such change is bad, but merely that it should be considered.

Economic development, as noted, is often advocated to relieve fiscal pressures. And, indeed, it often does. Yet it is also possible for the inmigration fostered by industrial or commercial development to make demands upon a municipality that cost more to satisfy than the new plant and the new residents contribute in revenues. If the increase in population pushes a municipality into major expansions of sewer and water systems, major construction of schools, and the provision of urban services not previously offered, the result may actually be a net fiscal loss. Occasionally, a seeming paradox occurs in which the newcomers pay more than their share of taxes and yet taxes still go up. If the incoming population has fundamentally different expectations of public services, it may change a once sleepy municipality from a low-tax/low-services situation to a high-tax/high-services situation. The result may be quite painful to some members of the original population. The old-timers will resent the new levels of expenditure, while the newcomers may feel entirely righteous because they are carrying their full share of the tax burden. This situation has been observed in suburban communities when the inmigrating population has been substantially wealthier than the native population. But there is no reason to believe it is confined to suburban areas.

None of the above side effects are cited as admonitions against economic development. The writer's experience, and what survey data are available, indicate that communities are, more often than not, pleased with the results of development programs. Rather, the effects are cited because they should be given serious consideration. Economic development will exact some prices, and these should be acknowledged and considered before deciding whether to embark upon a program. If the decision is to go ahead, then recognition of the side effects may make it possible to deal with them more effectively.

NOTES

1. "Tax expenditure" is a situation in which either an asset or a stream of income is treated in a more favorable manner than would normally be the case. Thus a property tax abatement, forgiveness on sales tax, a reduction in the corporate income tax for new industry, and the tax exemption for interest on IRBs are all tax expenditures.

2. See *Statistical Abstract of the United States: 1988*, Bureau of the Census, U.S. Department of Commerce, Washington, D.C., 1987, Table 475.

3. For a history of early local development efforts, see Alfred Eichner, *Development Agencies and Employment Expansion*, Wayne State University Press, Detroit, 1970.

4. At this writing both agencies are in much more precarious circumstances than when the first edition of this work was written. The Economic Development Administration (EDA) was funded at only about $200 million in fiscal 1989, and its fate in the 1990 budget cannot be predicted. The Reagan administration's executive budgets for a number of years attempted to "zero it out," but funds were appropriated by the Congress against administration wishes. The Urban Development Action Grant (UDAG) program in the 1989 fiscal year operated solely on $50 million in "recaptured" funds (monies appropriated for projects that did not materialize), and fresh appropriations for the 1990 fiscal year are not anticipated at this writing.

5. Wilbur Thompson, "Economic Processes and Employment Problems in Declining Metropolitan Areas," in *Post-Industrial America: Metropolitan Decline and Inter-Regional Job Shifts*, George Sternlieb and James W. Hughes, eds., Center for Urban Policy Research, Rutgers, State University of New Jersey, New Brunswick, 1975.

6. Wilbur Thompson, "Problems That Sprout in the Shadow of No-Growth," *Management and Control of Growth*, Vol. I, Randall W. Scott et. al., eds., Urban Land Institute, Washington, D.C., 1975, pp. 398–404.

2

The Political Context of Economic Development

In general, economic development programs have a very high degree of political visibility. A two-person economic development agency is likely to generate more press and media coverage than a much larger public-works department. Economic development activity is essentially newsworthy so far as local media are concerned. Plant openings and closings, promotional campaigns, and the relationship between tax ratables and the property-tax rate are of continuing interest to local residents. Not only is economic development activity newsworthy but, for reasons discussed in Chapter 9, media exposure is generally to be sought, not shunned.

Development agencies are often quite useful politically, and this is one reason they are created. Liberals and conservatives may disagree on whom to tax, how to tax, and what to spend. But they are likely to agree on a program that promises jobs to the working man and tax relief to the property owner. In a period when the public's esteem for government relative to the private sector is not especially high, economic development programs may enable government to borrow a certain amount of prestige. Rather than appearing as taxer and spender, government appears as a facilitator of beneficial private development. Local economic development is one government program that is popular in a politically conservative period.

The fact that local economic development activities are highly visible and often politically useful also makes them lightning rods for criticism. If the incumbent mayor or county executive created an economic development organization a year ago, his political opponent can criticize him because the organization he is funding out of the taxpayers' hard-earned money has yet to sign a single contract or bring in a single firm. If a firm moves out of the riety, public exposure, and a chance to be well known within a community. If one's efforts are successful, it offers considerable feelings of accomplishment. Often it pays well. But it is not a good choice for those who have particularly strong needs for security and stability.

THE DEVELOPMENT COALITION

One task for the recently formed development agency is building a coalition in favor of development. The economic developer who constructs such a coalition is more likely to be effective and will be better insulated against the vagaries of politics.

In most communities the essentials of a coalition for development are present and waiting for the economic developer. Property owners, in general, are likely to be for development because it holds out prospects for reduced tax burdens. Those who own property whose market value will rise as development increases demand have a second reason to favor development. This may be equally true of the owners of vacant land with commercial potential, of owners of stores and commercial buildings, and of apartment owners. Homeowners may perceive that economic growth increases the demand for housing, and that therefore they will ultimately profit from it. In the writer's experience, most businessmen are in favor of growth even when it does not serve their narrow interests. A local manufacturer, for example, is likely to favor economic development as a matter of principle even though it may tighten labor markets and increase his wage costs. The banking community is generally for development since it means more loan business. Commercial realtors are almost invariably for development for similar reasons. However, one must note here that their generally favorable development position may be tempered by fears that an active development agency may from time to time connect a buyer with a property owner directly, thus causing a broker to lose a commission.

Organized labor is almost inevitably for development and can be a major piece in the coalition for development. The only caution here is that the economic developer should reflect on whether the face his or her labor people will present to potential employers is one of cooperation and accommodation, or one of rigidity and hard-nosed militancy. If it is the former, they will be valuable allies; if it is the latter, their support is more to be desired from a distance than from close in.

Particularly in the early stages of a development agency's life, time spent acquainting these various constituencies with the agency's purposes and personnel is time well spent, even though it may show no immediate results.

In most communities, economic development will have some opponents, and it is well not to ignore them. Economic growth promotes change—physical, social, political. Some opposition to economic development will thus spring from this root. Opposition to economic development may come from expectations of increased traffic or increased population. In the suburban rings around major cities, economic development may be opposed because it brings with it the specter of urbanization. If the suburb is largely peopled by those who have come to it recently to escape the real or imagined evils of urban life, opposition on this count may be very strong.

In recent years, environmental consciousness has grown, and with it the strength of the environmental movement. This is true in terms of both political power and statutory authority. The general clash between the claims of environmental quality and economic need are by now well known. Much opposition to economic development will come from local environmental groups. Such opposition can be quite formidable. Local environmental groups often have a generally upper-middle-class membership that is politically well connected and articulate. Then, too, environmental groups often have a certain moral aura about them. Finally, environmental law is now sufficiently complex that litigation may delay a project for years, if not decades.

Where jurisdictions are small, opposition based on either planning or environmental issues may be particularly strong. This is because most of the benefit in terms of increased employment will accrue to people who live outside the municipality, whereas much of the traffic and environmental impact will occur within the municipality. Thus, many of those who would be for the project, but relatively few who are opposed, are politically disenfranchised.

The agency run by the writer in the late 1970s attempted to finance the development of a light-manufacturing firm in a municipality with an area of about two square miles. The municipality is part of the New York region, which, in less than a decade, had lost half a million manufacturing jobs. To the author and his agency, the virtue of the project seemed unarguable. Nonetheless, the agency ultimately had to back off and drop the project as a result of determined and skillfully organized citizen opposition. Opponents of the project pointed out that few of the firm's workers would live in the community and that, furthermore, few of the plant's workers would have the income even to contemplate buying a house in this predominantly middle- and upper-middle-class community. Few gains for local retailers were seen, for as one citizen opponent noted of the plant's presumed labor force, "Those are the kind of people who bring their lunch to work in a paper bag." Thus, community gains from the project seemed small, and what the author perceived as the regionwide gains carried little weight with community residents.

If opposition to economic development is likely to come from planning and environmental constituencies, what is the economic developer to do? In some cases, where there are uncompromisable differences between the goals of different groups, the matter will come down to a test of political strength or to judicial decision.

Nonetheless, the economic development agency may be able to minimize conflict and opposition by involving members of the potential opposition early on in the economic development process. For example, assume a citizen advisory board for an economic development agency is to be set up. One member of the board might be a prominent figure in the local environmental movement. This serves several purposes. First, it serves a mutual education function. The environmentalist on the board is exposed to the goals of the program and the needs the program seeks to meet. In due time, this exposure may create some rapport. If the environmentalist, for example, is a member of the upper middle class who has few blue-collar contacts, sitting next to a labor union leader may make him or her more sympathetic to the need for blue-collar jobs. Conversely, having an environmentalist on the board may make the board more conscious of the concerns of the environmental movement and of the real environmental costs of some projects. If a proposed project has serious environmental flaws, perhaps there may be room for some compromise and redesign. If potential conflicts can be discovered early, they can be discussed quietly, calmly, and privately. The chances of a mutually acceptable solution are far greater than if the same issues are aired late in the process in a public and highly political forum.

Similarly, there is a certain wisdom for including one or more representatives of what might be considered the planning or general public interest constituency in the development coalition. Again the goal is partly mutual education and partly early recognition of potential conflict. At one time, the writer was responsible for proposing the membership of the five-person board of a development financing agency. For one seat, he proposed a member of the planning establishment. The seat was filled by the chairman of the county planning board, an arrangement that worked very smoothly. Planning concerns were represented and, at the same time, the agency received some protection from charges that it was oblivious to the cause of good planning.

Apart from bringing members of the potential opposition into the process in a formal way, there is much to be said for informal communication. Ideally, this should begin before there is a specific bone of contention. In the early stages of an agency's existence, its personnel might hold conversations with environmentalists, planners, and representatives of such groups as the League of Women Voters, explaining the agency's goals and exploring areas of common interest and potential conflict. Such conversations open up a dialogue and avoid feelings of being ignored or of being surprised. Surprise is desirable for birthdays and anniversaries, but in the political world its most likely products are anger and opposition.

Obviously, economic developers must scrupulously respect the confidences of firms, property owners, brokers, and others with whom they have dealings. If they do not, their credibility will soon be gone and their capacity to do useful work destroyed. At the same time, to the extent that the potential opposition can be taken into the economic developers' confidence and included in the development process, opposition may be minimized and compromise furthered.

NOTE

1. The American Economic Development Council (formerly the American Industrial Development Council) does award a Certified Industrial Developer certificate on the basis of an examination. To take the exam, one must have five years of experience in the field. In addition, it requires either a college degree, completion of the Economic Development Institute program at the University of Oklahoma, or some additional years of field experience.

3

Organization and Personnel

Most development agencies, with the exception of chambers of commerce, either are parts of government or are closely allied with and at least partially funded by government. Thus we might begin by noting some characteristics of local economic development operations that are atypical of government. One theme of this volume is that local economic development is largely a sales operation. This is not the picture that is often presented in the academic literature on the subject, but the writer is absolutely convinced that it is true. As a quick, intuitive test of the proposition, the reader might consider attending a convention of local economic developers. The tone of the event and the personalities of the people will have an unmistakable sales feeling. It will not resemble a meeting of economists, regardless of the fact that the field is called "economic development." Economic development directors tend to be joiners. The director who belongs to Rotary, Lions, Kiwanis, a golf club, and a swim club, and coaches Little League in his spare time is fairly common. Aside from the fact that such activity often suits the extroverted personalities of many people in the field, economic development is a contact business. The greater one's web of acquaintances, the more effective one is likely to be. One young economic developer with a very good reputation mentioned to the writer that he belonged to two golf clubs in the New Jersey county where he worked, and felt that many of his best deals originated on the links.

In point of fact, someone who is a great economist but a poor salesman is not likely to make a good economic developer. On the other hand, many people who are good salesmen but have little formal knowledge of economics do very well in the field. The "selling" that local economic developers do is not the "smoke and mirrors" that sometimes sells consumer goods.

It is technical selling—highly factual and data intensive. But it is still selling. For most agencies most of the time, skill in dealing with people will be vastly more useful than skill at economic analysis.

Many economic development agencies perform an entrepreneurial role. They acquire land and develop industrial parks or downtown renewal sites. Or they may put up and market shell buildings. It is true that governments have long been engaged in acquiring land and building and operating facilities. But generally, governments build with a clear mission. The idea of building and then looking for a buyer or tenant is not the usual procedure for, say, a public works department.

Local economic development, then, is not the protypical government activity. That thought should be borne in mind when we turn to the matter of how an economic development agency fits into the structure of government.

DESIRABLE AGENCY CHARACTERISTICS

To think about the issue of how an agency might best be organized, let us list some desirable agency characteristics. Most of them are self-evident.

1. *Pro-business orientation.* You cannot successfully court someone you do not like. However, this should not mean a willingness to run rampant over the public interest in the cause of profit.

2. *Ability to respond rapidly.* Time is money, and many businesspeople, often with some justice, feel that people on the public side of the fence do not understand this.

3. *Access to the levers of government.* Public investment and the manner in which laws and regulations are implemented can be crucial to many projects. Access to the person or the agency that can make the decision, or compel someone else to make it, is very important.

4. *Technical ability.* How much ability an agency needs depends on its role and the extent to which it can depend on outsiders.

5. *Trustworthiness.* A reputation for trustworthiness is an agency's most valuable asset. If an agency loses credibility by its inability to keep confidences, or by making promises it cannot keep, it is largely disabled.

6. *Willingness to accept risk.* If the agency plays an entrepreneurial role or simply does some financing with the community's own funds, then willingness to take sensible risks is essential. Bureaucracies, by nature, are not generally risk takers. The system of rewards and punishments tends to discourage risk-taking behavior. The question of risk taking is important to bear in mind when thinking about how the economic development function is to be related to the rest of government.

TYPES OF ECONOMIC DEVELOPMENT ORGANIZATIONS

Most economic development organizations fit into one of the four categories below:

- *Public agencies.* These are agencies that are legally and administratively part of the structure of government. They may be line agencies, component parts of line agencies, or staff agencies. An example of the first type would be a separate department of economic development. An example of the second would be an economic development office included in a planning, community development, or public works department. An example of the third type might be an office of economic development attached to the office of a mayor, city manager, board of supervisors, or county executive. Typically, the line agency will have various operating responsibilities, whereas the staff agency will be essentially an advisory and a coordinating agency.

- *Semi-public agencies.* These may be public-benefit corporations or authorities. The common element is that they are created by a legislative act but are not part of the structure of government and have, at least in principle, some degree of autonomy. In addition to having the legal powers normally associated with private enterprises, such as the power to enter into contracts, such an organization may also have some powers normally associated with governments—for instance, the power to condemn land or to issue certain types of tax-exempt securities.

- *Private/public partnerships.* This category covers a very wide range. The organization may be a private entity, often organized as a not-for-profit corporation in which the public sector is represented through board membership. It may or may not have financial links to government, in that some part of its budget may come from the public treasury.

- *Purely private groups.* This category includes chambers of commerce and various city and county organizations. Funding is private, and there are no formal links to government.

Advantages and Disadvantages

The public agency may have the advantage so far as political access goes. This is particularly likely if it is organized in such a way that it is directly linked to the top of the political structure. A development agency that is organized as part of the mayor's office, or as a separate line agency reporting directly to that office, may be very well positioned to engage the interest of the political structure when required and to get quick answers from government when they are needed.

Such close linkage can also have its disadvantages. The operation can become so politicized that visibility becomes primary and actual accomplishment secondary. What appears in the press can become more important than what appears on the ground. Top positions in the agency may become filled with the politically deserving rather than the technically competent.

Well-paid and highly visible economic development jobs can make nice plums to offer campaign contributors, party loyalists, those with useful political connections, or those to whom one is indebted for services rendered in the political wars of days gone by.

The public agency, whether staff or line, may have certain difficulties with regard to personnel selection. If hiring and promotion must be done through a civil service structure, it may be difficult to get people with the right skills or the right private-sector background. Civil service tests are likely to be better at determining skills in typing or mathematics than in selling or public relations. Then, too, once someone gains a permanent appointment—generally after six months or a year—it is very difficult to discharge him or her if performance is not adequate.

Where the economic development group is lodged in a larger department, it may benefit from the technical and staff support of the larger agency. For example, a development group attached to a planning agency may benefit from the agency's data analysis, planning, and graphic capabilities, and perhaps, also, from the web of relationships the agency has built up with local officials over the years. On the other hand, the development group may find itself buried in an agency whose primary focus is otherwise, and it may thus find itself delayed and hampered when other agency goals take precedence. The same might be said for locating a development group in a major line agency like public works. The technical support may be useful at times, but the submergence of development concerns can be a definite problem. One economic development consultant with very wide experience notes, "It is a very bad idea to have those who do the regulating also do the promoting." Perhaps that is saying no more than "No man can serve two masters."

In the most general sense, the public agency, staff or line, and particularly line, may be troubled by the traditional problems of bureaucracy and civil service—excessive caution, red tape, and inflexibility.

The semi-public agency may avoid some of the problems of the public agency. Excessive politicization is less likely to occur. The greater freedom in hiring and firing that characterizes the private sector is likely to be an advantage. The semi-public agency or the private/public partnership agency may be capable of greater risk taking because its top people do not have to run for election. An unpaid board directing a semi-public agency has little to lose from behaving with a degree of boldness because they earn their livings elsewhere.

In fact, government may be able to use the semi-public agency as a stalking horse. The agency proposes a project. If public reaction is favorable, government allies itself with the project. If public reaction is unfavorable, government disavows the project or, in the extreme, joins the opposition.

A semi-public agency may also be very effective in building support for local economic development, in part because it is not so closely allied with government. This is particularly so in a conservative political environment. If the business community can be induced to put up some of the funding for a semi-public agency, a strong bond between business and the agency is created—the giving of funds constitutes an act of commitment. One development consultant of the author's acquaintance has, in fact, advised communities in some cases not to proceed with economic development programs if they cannot get some cash contribution from the business community.

The disadvantage of the semi-public agency is that, like all authorities, it is not under the same degree of public control as is a body of government. Accountability is limited. The agency may begin confusing its interests with those of the public in general. For example, there often are serious conflicts between economic development and environmental or planning considerations. What happens when a developer or investor wants to do what the agency (and perhaps everyone else) thinks is the right thing, in what the planners or the environmentalists are convinced is the wrong place?

The purely private organization, of which the chamber of commerce is the prototype, is usually not adequate to perform the full range of economic development activities. It may well be adequate for informational purposes, but not able to handle entrepreneurial and financing functions. Then, too, many chambers of commerce perform numerous business functions unrelated to economic development and thus may find it difficult to focus sufficient energy on the economic development task. The purely private agency may also lack adequate access to government, a potentially major limitation. Finally, the purely private agency may find that, from time to time, it must become preoccupied with supporting itself. The writer once observed a large regional chamber of commerce spending what seemed like an inordinate amount of time managing a track meet. When the writer asked the director why, the reply was very straightforward: "because we need the money."

Staffing Needs

Agency staffing needs, regardless of whether the agency is public, semi-public, or private, will vary with the types of things the agency does.

Virtually any agency has some public-relations side to its operation and needs someone who can handle that aspect of the operation. An agency staffed entirely by technical people, with no one who could address a Rotary club, or write a press release, or make follow-up phone calls after an advertising campaign would be quite handicapped, particularly in its early years. In fact, very often, development agencies begin by being staffed largely with front people and then take on more technical people as inquiries come in and projects begin to materialize.

How much technical depth the agency requires depends on what it does.

If the agency just serves a chamber-of-commerce function, but has no implementing or financing role, it may need only enough technical depth to build up a database and answer some general questions on matters like taxation, utilities, zoning, the structure of local government. City or regional planning often provides an excellent background for doing that type of work. If the agency is involved in financing, it is essential to have some legal and financial expertise available. The expertise may be contained within the staff or may be on tap on a consulting or an advisory basis. The writer once operated a revenue-bond-issuing agency whose ultimate financial and legal expertise resided, respectively, with two bankers on an unpaid board and with the agency's bond counsel. Full-time staff possessed enough understanding of financial and legal complexities to communicate with firms and to outline financial and legal arrangements in principle, but in no sense could be termed expert. The arrangement proved to be quite satisfactory.

If the agency actually performs a development function directly, meaning that it acquires property, markets parcels, and negotiates leases, then capabilities in commercial real estate and property management are essential. At least some of these capabilities should be available on a more or less full-time basis. Physical planning may be contracted out to a planning or engineering consultant because it can be done at one time, even though it may be periodically reviewed or monitored. If the agency is being formed as a branch of government that will have to hire under civil service rules, it is important to see that position titles, job descriptions, and the entire personnel process are set up in such a way that the agency will be able to hire people with usable backgrounds. The types of skills mentioned above are not likely to be found within the established civil service work force, and if the agency cannot break out of that structure for hiring purposes, it may be severely handicapped.

4

Recent Economic Changes

The economic landscape of the United States has changed rapidly in recent years, sometimes in bewildering ways. A good working grip on the main outlines of the "big picture" is essential for thinking about the larger questions of development strategy and marketing. Understanding the main currents of economic change will help the economic developer to distinguish between the inevitable, the possible, and the desirable-but-impossible—important distinctions to make when time, money, and legal and political powers are limited.

PATTERNS OF REGIONAL CHANGE

The shift of population and economic activity from the northeast and north central regions to the South and the West, the so-called Frostbelt/Sunbelt shift, has been widely recognized and widely documented for some years. As Table 4.1 indicates, the trend continued with considerable strength through the 1980s. Compare, for example, the 0.5 percent population growth in the east north central region with the 12.8 percent growth in the south Atlantic region and 14.9 percent in the Pacific coast region.

The causes of the regional shifts are generally well recognized. The most obvious is that the nation was first settled in the Northeast, and diffusion will naturally take place from that region. Climate is an important factor and has been exerting a southward pull for decades.

For the deep South and Southwest that pull has been greatly strengthened by the development of air conditioning in the years since World War II. The building of the interstate highway system, the development of electronic communications, and the expansion of both scheduled and non-

Table 4.1
Regional Change in the 1980s

Region	Population in 1987	Percent change from 1980	Non-Agri-cultural employ-ment in 1986	Percent change from 1980	Manufact-uring em-ployment in 1986	Percent change from 1980
U.S.	243,400	7.4	99,610	10.1	18,994	-6.4
N.E.	12,884	4.0	6,224	13.6	1,405	-7.7
M.A.	37,433	1.8	16,187	7.8	2,992	-16.0
E.N.C.	41,904	.5	17,134	2.4	4,148	-12.0
W.N.C.	17,634	2.6	7,237	4.8	1,297	-24.1
S.A.	41,684	12.8	17,383	18.3	3,082	-4.6
E.S.C	15,290	4.3	5,516	7.3	1,325	-2.9
W.S.C.	26,910	13.1	10,058	8.0	1,502	-9.6
Mt.	13,167	15.8	5,184	15.1	603	+6.9
Pac.	36,533	14.9	14,758	12.9	2,599	+6.3

Notes: Employment figures exclude proprietors, the self-employed, military personnel, domestic workers, and unpaid family workers.

Geographic divisions are as follows: New England (Maine, New Hampshire, Vermont, Massachusetts, Rhode Island, Connecticut); Middle Atlantic (New York, New Jersey, Pennsylvania); East North Central (Ohio, Indiana, Illinois, Michigan, Wisconsin); West North Central (Minnesota, Iowa, Missouri, North Dakota, South Dakota, Nebraska, Kansas); South Atlantic (Delaware, Maryland, District of Columbia, Virginia, West Virginia, North Carolina, South Carolina, Georgia, Florida); East South Central (Kentucky, Tennessee, Alabama, Mississippi); West South Central (Arkansas, Louisiana, Oklahoma, Texas); Mountain (Montana, Idaho, Wyoming, Colorado, New Mexico, Arizona, Utah, Nevada); Pacific (Washington, Oregon, California, Hawaii, and Alaska).

Source: Statistical Abstract of the United States, 102nd and 108th editions.

scheduled aviation have reduced the relative isolation of formerly remote areas and thus lessened the locational advantages of the northeast and north central regions. The growth of a large senior citizen population with substantial "mailbox income" has permitted millions of people to migrate south and west from the Frostbelt. Their buying power creates jobs and thus promotes the migration of younger people as well. It is no coincidence that from 1980 to 1987 the three fastest-growing states in the "lower 48" were Arizona, Florida, and Nevada. As the table indicates, trends in both total employment and manufacturing employment have generally paralleled population trends. This is not surprising, for population growth builds local markets and thus promotes employment growth. Conversely, new job opportunities promote inmigration.

THE GROWTH IN U.S. FOREIGN TRADE

International trade is a crucial part of the picture for the economic developer. As Table 4.2 indicates, international trade has grown steadily as a percentage of gross national product (GNP). The United States, in absolute dollar amounts, is the world's largest exporter and importer. In terms of both threats and opportunities, international trade cannot be ignored. The major causes of the growth of U.S. international trade are well known:

Table 4.2
The Growth of U.S. Merchandise Trade as a Share of GNP

Year	Merchandise trade as a percent of GNP
1950	3.5
1955	3.4
1960	3.4
1965	3.5
1970	4.1
1975	6.5
1980	8.5
1985	7.0
1987	7.3

Notes: Figures are the average of imports and exports divided by GNP. Figures are for merchandise only and do not include services.

Sources: Data through 1985 from *Statistical Abstract of the United States,* various editions. Data for 1987 from *Economic Indicators,* Joint Economic Council, U.S. Government Printing Office, Washington, D.C., November 1988.

1. Decreases in the time and cost of transportation and communication.

2. Decreases in tariff and nontariff barriers under the General Agreement on Trade and Tariffs (GATT). In the 1930s the average tariff on U.S. imports was equal to about 60 percent of the value of the good. By the 1970s this figure had fallen to about 5 percent.

3. The development of huge, highly effective international capital markets. In the age of the microchip, capital can travel with the speed of light.

4. U.S. foreign policy since World War II. In 1945, with Germany and Japan occupied and the U.S. allies exhausted by war, the United States enjoyed a position of economic dominance. Rather than exploit this position, the United States chose to help both former enemies and allies get back on their feet as quickly as possible. The very benevolent occupation of Germany and Japan, the Marshall Plan, GATT, and the formation of the International Monetary Fund and the World Bank had the effect of restoring damaged economies and facilitating the resumption and acceleration of world trade. We have helped to rebuild former allies and former enemies, both as competitors and as markets for U.S. exports.

5. The accelerated diffusion of scientific knowledge and technology since World

War II. This diffusion has facilitated the development of powerful manufacturing and trading economies in various parts of the world. In the Pacific rim the combination of Western levels of technological skill and distinctly sub-Western wage levels has produced new and very formidable competitors. Most notable among these at present are Taiwan and South Korea. Hong Kong and Singapore have also become formidable, though smaller, trading powers. At this writing Thailand appears to be experiencing the beginnings of economic takeoff. Relatively low-technology products from the People's Republic of China (clothing, simple electronics) are beginning to show up on the shelves of U.S. mass merchandisers. It would be foolish to underestimate Chinese potential either as a major exporter or as a major market. Recent rates of economic growth in China suggest that that nation may very soon be a major factor in world trade.

Japan, whose economic takeoff preceded those of other Asian nations by at least half a century, competes on a different basis. Japanese wage levels are comparable with Western levels. The Japanese compete, instead, on the basis of technical virtuosity, a very effective form of internal economic organization and a trade policy that in some ways is reminiscent of a pre-Adam Smith mercantilism.[1]

THE TRADE DEFICIT

The trade deficit and what it may imply about the prospects for U.S. manufacturing industries was the subject of much discussion during the 1980s. In particular, the question at issue was whether the trade deficits of the 1980s implied a fundamental competitive weakness on the part of U.S. industry. Table 4.3 shows major trends in U.S. exports, imports, and the value of the dollar against a bundle of major currencies during the 1980s. Recall in looking at the figures that the nation emerged from recession in 1982 and at this writing (early 1990) is entering the eighth year of an economic expansion, the longest in U.S. peacetime history. As the table indicates, U.S. exports declined slightly early in the decade, were relatively flat for several years, and then rose sharply in the later part of the decade. From 1985 through 1988 the value of U.S. exports rose by about 50 percent. For imports, the pattern was quite different. Imports remained relatively flat for the first few years of the decade, but after 1983 began a very sharp climb. As of 1988 they were still growing rapidly. The value of the dollar as measured against the currencies of other major trading nations rose steadily from the beginning of the decade, peaking in early 1985. It then began a rapid decline; by early 1988, it was almost down to its 1980 level.

In the view of many economists, much of the trade picture shown in the table can be explained in terms of the two macroeconomic events noted above: the sustained economic boom and the very large fluctuations of the dollar. An economic boom increases the volume of imports simply because domestic demand rises. However, it does not necessarily stimulate exports. In fact, a strong domestic market may distract manufacturers from pursuing export sales. The rise in the value of the dollar from 1980 to 1985 placed foreign firms at an advantage in the U.S. market. This effect, combined with strong domestic demand, appears to explain much of the remarkable increase in imports during the first half of the 1980s. The flatness of U.S. exports in the same period is, in large measure, explained by the strength of the dollar, which made U.S. goods more expensive in overseas market. In fact, one might well be surprised that U.S. exports held up as well as they did in the face of such steep increases in the value of the dollar. The sharp uptrend in U.S. exports after 1986 was largely due to the weakening of the

Table 4.3
U.S. International Trade Since 1982 (figures in billion dollars)

| | -------Exports--------- | | --------Imports------- | | Relative value of the dollar 1977=100 |
	Total merch.	Mfg. Goods	Total merch.	Mfg. Goods	
1980	224.3	-----	249.8	-----	82
1981	237.1	-----	265.1	-----	87
1982	216.4	102.7	244.0	108.4	102
1983	205.6	97.4	258.0	126.6	114
1984	224.0	105.9	325.7	173.3	128
1985	218.8	109.4	345.3	200.2	146
1986	227.2	111.7	365.4	229.4	119
1987	254.1	127.9	406.2	258.4	98
1988	322.4	161.6	441.0	285.0	91

The manufactured goods figures are the sum of the categories Capital Goods except Automotive; Automotive Vehicles, Parts, and Engines; and Consumer Goods (nonfood) except Automotive. They omit the categories Industrial Supplies and Materials, and Other. Both categories include some manufactured goods. Thus both exported and imported manufactures are understated. The understatement is probably greater for exports. The 1980 and 1981 figures are on a somewhat different basis than earlier figures, and therefore no breakout of manufactured goods is given. The dollar values are figured against a bundle of the currencies of Belgium, Canada, France, Germany, Italy, Japan, the Netherlands, Sweden, Switzerland, and the United Kingdom. The figures are for January of the year shown. The figures can be interpreted as saying that the value of the dollar rose relative to the bundle of ten currencies by 78 percent from 1980 to 1985 and then declined 31 percent from that peak to 1988.

Source: The trade figures are from *Economic Indicators,* Council of Economic Advisors, U.S. Government Printing Office, Washington, D.C., various months. The dollar values are from various issues of *December Survey of Current Business,* U.S. Department of Commerce, Washington, D.C.

dollar. Imports continued strong after 1986 but they grew less rapidly than exports. Table 4.3 shows the pattern through 1988. In the first three quarters of 1989 exports of manufactured goods grew by 15.0 percent while imports of manufactured goods grew by only 7.4 percent. Note that patterns of trade take time to adjust to changes in currency valuations. For a time foreign producers may adapt to weakening of the dollar by reducing profits or even taking losses in order to retain market share. The Japanese, who are noted for taking the long view, are particularly prone to this. The high degree of vertical integration in Japanese industry and the close links between firms and banks give many Japanese producers the financial strength to put market share above short-term profitability.

It is often asserted that the U.S. trade deficit is a major cause of job losses in manufacturing. How valid is this allegation? At this writing the trade deficit on manufactured goods is in the range of $100 billion annually. Value added in manufacturing, as shown in Table 4.4, is in the $1,000 billion range, and the total value of all goods manufactured in the United States is about $2,000 billion (about half of the value of manufactured goods is produced outside of the manufacturing sector: raw materials, energy, transportation, services, and so on). Manufacturing employment in the United States is currently in the 19 million range. The trade deficit is thus roughly equivalent to 10 percent of value added in manufacturing and 5 percent of the total value of U.S. manufactures. As a quick estimate, then, between 1 and 2 million jobs in U.S. manufacturing would be regained if the manufacturing trade deficit were totally erased.

While a manufacturing trade deficit of the size the United States experienced in the mid-1980s is hardly trivial, one might still ask why it has created quite so much alarm as it has. The answer lies, in large measure, in the pattern of imports and exports. The three categories of manufactured goods in which the United States runs its largest trade deficits are, in order of size, automobiles, consumer durables, and clothing. These are highly visible items in everyday life. On the other hand, the United States is a major net exporter of chemicals and aircraft and at this writing also runs a small surplus on capital goods (it is the world's largest importer and exporter in this category). But these categories are not nearly so visible in everyday life. Another factor that adds to the perception of calamity is geographic concentration. Both steel and automobile manufacturing are concentrated in the north central region of the country, and the images of shuttered mills and unemployed workers in these areas are powerful indeed.

INDUSTRIAL CHANGE AND THE
DEINDUSTRIALIZATION CONTROVERSY

With the penetration of U.S. markets for automobiles, bicycles, consumer electronics, and other manufactured products, there has been much discussion of deindustrialization.[2] Table 4.4 shows some overall annual manufacturing statistics for the United States for the period 1949–87. As the table indicates, total employment in manufacturing has remained relatively stable. Thus, in an absolute sense it is hard to make the case that the United States is deindustrializing.

Table 4.4
U.S. Manufacturing, 1949–89

Year	Total mfg. emp. (millions)	Mfg. prod. emp. (millions)	Value added in mfg. as % of GNP	Value added in mfg. in current dollars (billions)	Value added in mfg. in 1972 dollars (billions)
1949	13.9	11.0	29.3	75.4	139.3
1951	14.8	12.5	31.1	102.1	174.2
1953	17.1	13.5	33.3	121.7	201.4
1955	16.8	13.0	33.1	135.0	219.2
1957	17.1	12.8	32.6	147.8	221.6
1961	16.3	11.8	31.6	164.3	229.4
1963	16.9	12.3	32.6	192.1	261.7
1965	18.0	13.1	33.1	226.9	299.0
1967	19.4	14.0	32.8	262.0	325.4
1969	20.0	14.4	32.7	304.4	347.1
1971	18.4	12.9	29.7	314.1	324.2
1973	19.9	14.2	30.9	405.6	383.4
1975	18.3	12.6	29.1	442.5	351.7
1977	19.6	13.7	30.5	585.2	417.7
1979	21.0	14.5	30.9	747.5	457.4
1981	20.3	13.5	28.4	837.5	428.2
1983	18.7	12.2	26.7	882.0	409.7
1985	18.8	12.2	25.0	999.1	432.7
1986	18.4	11.8	24.5	1035.4	436.8
1987	19.1	----	----	-----	-----
1988	19.4	----	----	-----	-----
1989	19.6(pr)	----	----	-----	-----

Sources: Through 1986 figures on manufacturing employment and value added are from U.S. Department of Commerce, Annual Survey of Manufacturing, 1986, Table 1a. These have been converted to 1972 dollars in the rightmost column, using the GNP deflator. The 1986 through 1989 total manufacturing employment figures are from U.S. Department of Commerce, *Economic Indicators*, January 1990.

On the other hand, manufacturing employment as a percent of total employment is shrinking, and has been doing so for many years. A small part of this shrinkage in the last several years has been due to import competition, but most of it appears to be inevitable. Productivity in manufacturing has grown more rapidly than productivity in the economy as a whole.

Thus, unless manufactured goods were to compose an increasing share of the GNP, a most unlikely scenario for a mature economy, shrinkage in manufacturing employment as a share of total employment is inevitable.

Manufacturing has absorbed, and will continue to absorb, a large share of the economic developer's attention. Its relative footlooseness compared with, say, retailing or personal services makes this inevitable. However, the economic developer should be aware that regardless of what happens with regard to foreign trade, manufacturing is likely to continue shrinking as a percentage of total employment. Thus some redirection of attention to other sectors would seem to make sense.

While manufacturing has shown stability in total employment, there has been considerable change in the composition of the manufacturing sector, as shown in Table 4.5.

Table 4.5
Changes in Manufacturing Employment, 1967–85 (figures in thousands)

SIC	Name	1967	1985	Percent change
20	Food and kindred	1,725	1,545	-10.4
21	Tobacco	83	64	-22.9
22	Textiles	954	688	-27.9
23	Apparel	1,372	1,099	-19.9
24	Lumber	562	632	+12.5
25	Furniture	430	484	+12.6
26	Paper	671	637	-5.1
27	Printing & Publ.	1,052	1,415	+34.5
28	Chemicals	983	1,046	+6.4
29	Petrochem & coal	211	193	-8.5
30	Rubber & misc. plast.	531	775	+46.0
31	Leather goods	337	155	-54.0
32	Stone, clay, glass	621	557	-10.3
33	Primary metals	1,329	774	-41.8
34	Fabricated metals	1,375	1,523	+10.8
35	Machy except elec	1,929	2,133	+10.6
36	Elec. & electronic	1,981	2,206	+11.4
37	Transport equip.	1,936	1,862	-3.8
38	Instruments	410	662	+61.5
39	Misc.	832	334	-59.9
	TOTAL	19,323	18,791	-2.8

Notes: Figures include administrative and auxiliary workers. SIC 35 includes computers for historic reasons going back to the days of the hand-cranked adding machine. Figures do not add to totals due to rounding.

Source: Annual Survey of Manufacturing, 1985, U.S. Department of Commerce, Table 2.

A number of clear winners and losers are visible. Among the big losers are Textiles, Apparel, Leather Goods, Primary Metals (mostly the steel industry), and the Miscellaneous category. Among the winners are Printing and Publishing, Rubber and Miscellaneous Plastics, Machinery except Electric, Electrical and Electronic Equipment, and Instruments. This pattern of winners and losers is not difficult to explain. Textiles and Apparel are relatively labor-intensive industries that produce goods with a high value per pound. The major penetration of U.S. markets by overseas producers seems inevitable in this age of low tariffs and good transportation. The losses in Leather Goods represent a mixture of import competition and technological change (note the corresponding increase in Rubber and Miscellaneous Plastics).

The biggest and best-known loser is Primary Metals. One factor here is simply that the demand for steel has been flattening out. Substitute materials and the redesign of many products have moderated the demand for steel. For example, the average U.S. automobile is about half a ton lighter than it was in the early 1970s. That alone translates into perhaps 5 million tons less steel consumed per year. Import competition has also been a big factor. For many years the steel industry was able to pass on very generous wage increases to the consumer. Steelworkers were among the best-paid industrial workers in the United States, which rendered the steel industry highly vulnerable to import competition. This vulnerability was exacerbated by world overcapacity in steel. At present, the U.S. steel industry is healthy and profitable. In the last several years productivity has been rising at about 5 percent a year. But employment in the industry is down to not much more than half its all-time peak. Even if U.S. steel imports fell to zero, the combination of rising productivity and flattening demand would prevent employment from reaching the levels that prevailed in the 1970s.

A somewhat similar story can be told with regard to automobiles. Job losses in automobile manufacture are not evident in Table 4.5 because automobile manufacturing is contained in the Transportation Equipment category, which, as a whole, has done well. At present, the U.S. automobile industry is healthy. Approximately 15 million vehicles of all types were produced in 1988 and profits were strong. General Motors showed profits of over $4 billion. However, the alarming penetration of U.S. automobile markets in recent years, particularly by the Japanese, has forced U.S. producers to spend billions on automated facilities. The result has been decreases in employment as a result of greatly increased productivity. "Outsourcing" (the purchase of components from distant producers) and joint production agreements have also cut employment.

The Miscellaneous category is hard to specify, but it includes a number of industries, such as costume jewelry, which are labor intensive and in which U.S. high-tech capabilities do not make up for major labor-cost differentials.

The biggest winner is Printing and Publishing. Demand has been growing, productivity growth has not matched the increase in demand, and import competition has not been a major problem. The growth in Plastics and

Rubber represents, in large measure, technological change. The Machinery except Electric category is something of a misnomer. For historic reasons it includes computers, an area in which the United States, in spite of formidable Japanese competition, is very strong. The remaining two categories, Electric and Electronic Machinery, and Instruments, suggest the ability to compete quite well in high-technology fields. Capital intensity per se does not seem to be a good predictor of U.S. competitive ability. The United States is a net exporter in Chemicals and a net importer in Primary Metals. Both industries have very high capital-to-worker ratios.

Reasoning from simple, commonsense principles, it is possible to construct a general scenario for change in the composition of manufacturing that is consistent with the data in Table 4.5. We know that manufacturing technology has spread across many parts of the world with great speed, and that flow shows no sign of slackening. We also know that transportation and communication costs have fallen greatly in recent decades. Under GATT we have seen a remarkable disassembling of trade barriers. Finally, we know that there are enormous wage differences between the United States and many countries that have mastered modern manufacturing technologies. However, we also know that overall productivity in manufacturing in the United States is probably as high as that of any other nation, and that there are broad areas of basic research and technology in which the United States is still either predominant or among the very few top nations. Putting it all together, we can visualize a scenario in which the United States retains industry in the categories listed below but experiences some losses in categories outside this list.

1. Products that must be used within a short time after production (newspapers).

2. Products that have such low value per pound that they cannot be economically shipped long distances (cement).

3. Products at the very edge of technology in which the United States has a clear lead (commercial and military aircraft, genetically engineered pharmaceuticals, fiber optic communications devices).

4. Products that are primarily produced by advanced economies whose labor costs are not radically different from those of the United States. In that case relatively small differences in productivity and fluctuations in exchange rates would render the game more or less a toss-up. At this writing, office machinery, many types of computers, and automobiles would fall into this category. The argument really is that by the time a nation's economy has reached the level of maturity which enables it to produce a wide range of complex, state-of-the-art goods, its labor costs are at or rapidly approaching First World levels.

5. Products that are so capital intensive that labor costs become trivial. It is hard to name an example now, but with the coming of highly automated production systems that may cost $500,000 or more per worker, such classes of products may become apparent.

6. Military products that, as a matter of law or policy, must be domestically produced. There is a large overlap here with category 3.

Item 4 on the list is far from trivial. The bulk of trade for most developed nations is with other developed nations. The United States' biggest trading partner is Canada. Japan is second, and the nations of Western Europe, taken together, are third. If one subtracts a single commodity, oil, the share of U.S. trade outside of the developed nations is relatively small.

Though it is not evident from the tables, one final point about manufacturing location should be noted. In the years after World War II, southern and western states often profited from the loss of industrial jobs in the North.[3] Improved communications and the building of the interstate highway system reduced the locational disadvantages of these regions and enabled them to convert advantages of cost and climate into rapid industrial growth. This growth was often aided by a pro-business political climate, active recruitment of firms, and generous financial incentives. It was not a matter of large numbers of northern firms simply packing up and moving, but the net effect was often the same. A northern firm might open a branch in a southern location. If that proved more profitable, it might gradually shift the bulk of its investment in new capacity to the new plant. Years later, if the new location were much more profitable, it might close its operation in the original location. This sort of process is not entirely over, but the economic developer who hangs his or her hat solely on labor and other cost differentials is nonetheless playing a risky game in this age of greatly expanded international trade.

OFFSHORING, JOINT PRODUCTION, AND REVERSE INVESTMENT

U.S. manufacturing is becoming internationalized in a variety of ways of which the economic developer should be aware. An increasing number of products are neither domestic nor imported but a hybrid of the two. The economist's principle of comparative advantage suggests that in an environment of free trade, nations will specialize in those products in which they have a comparative or relative advantage. It has turned out that this principle can, and often does, operate at the subproduct level. Components are made and operations performed at the most efficient location and the "made in ____" label may not tell much more than where the final assembly took place. The IBM PC on which this manuscript was typed is made in the United States by a U.S. company, but a quick look at the components inside indicates that it is actually an international product. The fact that a substantial part of Mexico's manufacturing establishment is massed along the Rio Grande is an indication of this internationalization of manufacturing. Products and components move across the border on the basis of relative costs in a pattern that may be bewildering but is fundamentally more efficient than a system which required that a product be all Mexican or all American. In some cases, this sharing of production may be done with products that are quite simple. For example, a producer of rubber gloves ships the latex from the United States to a Mexican plant that forms the latex into gloves and ships the finished product back across the border. The U.S. comparative advantage in chemicals is combined with the Mexican comparative advantage in the more labor-intensive parts of the operation.

Much attention has been focused on joint production agreements, particularly between U.S. and Japanese firms. A very common arrangement is that the R&D and initial product development is done in the United States, much of the more complex manufacturing is done in Japan, and final assembly and packaging is done in the United States.[4] Some writers have complained that the Japanese have generally gotten the better end of this arrangement. In effect, the United States has gotten the head and the tail, with the Japanese getting the carcass with most of the meat. This may well be true, and at some point legislation changing the rules of the game may be forthcoming. However, for the economic developer the immediate task is to understand the situation so as to play the game as well as possible under the existing rules.

The economic developer should be aware of the very large amount of reverse investment that is occurring in the United States. Reverse investment is fueled from several sources. The trade deficits of the last few years have produced a major increase in the number of dollars in foreign hands. Many of these dollars return as reverse investment in buildings, land, and production facilities. Its political stability and the size its markets make the United States a very attractive location for many investors. The decline in the value of the dollar since 1985 has made U.S. assets even more attractive. Reverse investment also is a path around both tariff and nontariff trade barriers. Toyotas built in a U.S. facility are not blocked by domestic-content legislation. Finally, having a foot in the United States gives a foreign producer some insurance against exchange rate fluctuations. For example, when the yen traded at 180 to the dollar, Japanese cars in the United States were high-quality products available at modest prices. When the yen trades at 120 to the dollar Japanese-made cars are still high-quality products, but they sell at premium prices. The result is likely to be either reduced market share or reduced profit margins. Owning a U.S. plant is a way around this dilemma that has proven very attractive to Japanese automakers. Again, regardless of how one feels about the trend and about rules or lack of rules regulating reverse investment, the immediate task for the economic developer is to play by the existing rules. That means that prospecting for reverse investment may well be an important part of the community's marketing plan. Since overseas marketing operations are likely to be prohibitively expensive for most communities, the obvious move is to take maximum advantage of state operations and, in effect, achieve some economies of scale in marketing.

LOOKING AHEAD

There has been so much change since the first edition of this book was written that one is hesitant to make predictions. But one can suggest some events in the offing that the economic developer might keep an eye on. In Europe the Economic Community is scheduled to achieve complete abolition of internal barriers to the flow of goods, labor, and capital in 1992. How this will play out in world trade cannot be foretold. The absence of internal barriers and differences in law and regulation from one nation to the other may make Europe more open for some U.S. exporters. On the other hand, the formation of a single trading area with roughly the economic mass of the United States may cause or permit the Europeans to turn inward and become more restrictive to the outside world at the same time they become less restrictive with each other. Without hazarding any guesses, let us simply note that for the economic developer with an international focus, 1992 is a year to keep in mind.

Another date to keep in mind is 1998, the year the United States/Canada Free Trade Agreement is fully implemented. The complete abolition of international barriers will turn the entire continent north of the Rio Grande into a single free trade area. Given the relative sizes of the United States and Canada, the effect on the Canadian economy will inevitably be greater. Nonetheless, there will be effects on U.S. firms. For some the dropping of barriers will mean improved access to Canadian markets. For others it will mean increased threats from Canadian producers. Whether Mexico will some day join the United States/Canada free trade area remains to be seen, just as it remains to be seen whether some Eastern European nations, now that Comecon and the Warsaw Pact appear to be coming apart, will assume partial or full membership in the Economic Community. The formation of a Pacific trading bloc with Japan dominant, or at least first among equals, would not be surprising. In any case, the creation of vast free trade areas and the possible formation of great, multination trading blocs is worth noting.

Another item for the internationally minded economic developer to keep at the periphery of his or her vision is the debt crisis. In the 1970s generous (perhaps very ill-advised) lending by Western banks enabled many Third World countries, including Mexico, Argentina, and Brazil, to pile up huge amounts of debt that, at this writing, they cannot service. What will be done about Third World debt in the way of forgiveness, rollovers, and interest writedowns remains to be seen. With the debt crisis has come some drying up of potential markets for U.S. manufacturers, particularly in the western hemisphere. To the extent that the crisis is resolved and Third World countries are able to follow more expansive monetary and fiscal policies, substantial markets for U.S.-made capital and consumer goods will open up. At that time states and cities which now have trade offices in London, Brussels, or Tokyo may find that offices in Mexico City, Buenos Aires, or São Paulo also make good sense.

NOTES

1. For an account of how Japanese trade policy and industrial and commercial organization contribute to Japanese trade prowess, see Clyde V. Prestowitz, *Trading Places: How We Allowed Japan to Take the Lead*, Basic Books, New York, 1988. Prestowitz' views are hardly universal, but he is very well informed and the book is well worth reading.

2. There has been a very lively debate on the subject of whether deindustrialization is a fact. Analyzing that debate would require far more space than is available here. For an optimistic view, see Robert Z. Lawrence, *Can America Compete*, The Brookings Institution, Washington, D.C., 1984. For a more alarmed view, see Stephen S. Cohen and John Zysman, *Manufacturing Matters: The Myth of the Post-Industrial Economy*, Basic Books, New York, 1987. In the same vein, see Prestowitz, *Trading Places*. For an interesting and diametrically opposed set of articles, see George Gilder, "The Revitalization of Everything: The Law of the Microcosm," *Harvard Business Review*, March–April 1988, pp. 49–61; and Charles H. Ferguson, "From the People Who Brought You VooDoo Economics," *Harvard Business Review*, May–June 1988. See also John E. Schwarz and Thomas J. Volgy, "The Myth of America's Economic Decline," *Harvard Business Review*, September–October 1985, p. 98.

3. Casting the matter in north/south terms oversimplifies it. The metropolitan/nonmetropolitan distinction was equally important. In general, nonmetropolitan area wages are lower than metropolitan area wages. The migration alluded to in text was often also a migration to a nonmetropolitan area; for example, from a northern city to a southern nonmetropolitan area such as the Piedmont area of Virginia or North Carolina.

4. See Robert Reich, *Tales of a New America*, Vantage Books, New York, 1987, ch. 4.

5

The Role of the States

Since the first edition of this work was written at the beginning of the 1980s, the role of the states in local economic development has greatly increased. Because the states are now bigger players of the game than formerly, it is all the more important that the economic developer be thoroughly conversant with his or her state's programs.

Several reasons are generally cited for the growing state role. One is the cutback in federal aid to the states under the Reagan administration's "new federalism." This forced the states to do more on their own. In this sense, the states' growing activism in economic development is part of a larger pattern of increased scope and competence of state government. Another reason for the increased state presence is the greater role of world trade in the U.S. economy and, specifically, the penetration of U.S. markets by overseas producers. Most city, town, or county agencies are not big enough to do many of the things that are required to compete in a world of large, distant rivals. Still another reason for increased state activism is regional economic change. In the east and north central regions, job losses in manufacturing, particularly those associated with steel and autos, made it apparent that some sort of larger-scale strategy was necessary. In its absence economic development efforts would simply consist of increasingly sharp competition over slices of a steadily shrinking pie. Finally, there is an emulation effect. The fact that one state starts what appears to be an enlightened, progressive program pushes other states to follow it. The Massachusetts venture capital program, begun in the late 1970s, naturally encouraged other states to offer similar programs. Apart from the fact that it seemed like a good idea, no politician likes to be asked, "How come they are doing such and such and we aren't?"

Traditionally, the explicit state presence in economic development often amounted to a variety of tax preferences for new investment, loan guarantee and interest rate reduction programs, some manpower training programs, and a marketing effort run through the Department of Commerce or other state agency. The latter typically was designed to draw attention to the state in general, with the state agency then furnishing leads to local agencies. Follow-up was, and is, largely a matter of local agency initiative. In fact, were state officials to become overly directive in steering inquiring firms to particular jurisdictions, howls of protest from bypassed jurisdictions would soon put a stop to the practice.

The various investment credits, corporate income tax reductions, and the like offered by state governments are not nearly such powerful factors as more basic items like market access and labor force quality. However, when these larger factors are more or less evenly balanced, financial incentives may be decisive. As in chess, when most of the bigger pieces are gone from the board, a pawn may decide the game.

State manpower training programs can be a useful recruiting tool. Typically, the state will fund training that is specifically keyed to the needs of the firm. Such programs are not likely to be the dominant factor in the location decision, but they are of some direct importance and are very reassuring about the attitude of the state. The "we will train your workers in the skills that you need" approach lacks the social virtues of a manpower training program that is targeted to the disadvantaged. On the other hand, it is likely to be more effective as a recruitment device because it is aimed directly at the firm's operational needs.

The implicit, but vital, state role in local economic development is public capital investment, for access to labor and access to markets are two of the prime determinants of business location. One of the big economic development triumphs of recent years was Tennessee's attraction of the General Motors Saturn facility to Spring Hill, south of Nashville. The basic factors that swung GM's decision are generally considered to be centrality of location, wage rates, and labor force quality. The state did not offer tax incentives, as some competing states did. However, a vital part of the understanding with GM was that the state would provide necessary highway and utility improvements. In 1979 the state had attracted Nissan, the Japanese motor vehicle maker. The plant originally made small trucks but is now making automobiles as well. A vital part of the understanding was the commitment for state expenditures of $11 million in road improvements in the vicinity of the site.[1]

In recent years the sums of money expended by states on behalf of major corporate relocations have become surprisingly large. The states' offerings typically include infrastructure expenditures and tax concessions. They may also include loans, loan guarantees, land, some absorption of site preparation costs, and expenditures for job training, among others. According to

Guskind, Illinois offered a $183 million package in 1985 to get a Chrysler-Mitsubishi plant. The state had offered a $200 million package in an unsuccessful attempt to get the GM Saturn plant noted above. Perhaps most surprising, the state spent $178 million simply to keep a Sears, Roebuck and Co. merchandising operation in the state. The facility employed 6,000 workers. The cost to the state was thus almost $30,000 per job.[2]

In these megadeals the advantage clearly lies with the firm. A large production, distribution, or administration of a national or international firm may have a choice of sites in many different states. It does not take very much effort on the part of the firm to initiate a bidding war between the states. In a bargaining sense the firm holds all the high cards. It has numerous choices and it knows its own motivations, plans, and cost considerations better than any outsider can. In talking to representatives of one state it can exaggerate the offers made by other states. It can bluff. If Governor Thompson of Illinois had thought that Sears was bluffing and would not have moved in any case, he might have been putting his political life on the line by calling that bluff. Perhaps Sears could have been kept in Illinois with an offer of only $100 million. But better to offer as much as possible than try to save the taxpayers' money, lose the firm, and then have to answer all those embarrassing political questions beginning with "Why didn't you . . ."

It is hard to believe that the bidding war between the states has not passed the point at which the public interest is best served and is now moving into a realm which the treasuries of many states can ill afford. We take up the question of the efficiency effects of subsidization in chapter 13.

In recent years many new types of state activity have been added and more traditional programs have been strengthened. Numerous states have begun venture capital programs. "Venture capital" is not a precisely defined term, but generally it means financing for start-up businesses that hold the prospect of large returns but cannot obtain adequate conventional financing. Often the provider of venture capital takes an equity position in the firm (becomes part owner of the firm). Thus, in addition to interest or dividend payments, there is a chance for capital gains. It is that prospect for capital gains which makes the venture capitalist willing to lend in risky situations. An occasional big winner compensates for the inevitable defaults.

Venture capital was a big force behind the growth of the semiconductor and genetic engineering industries, where there were numerous new firms that were long on brains and ideas but short on traditional balance sheet items. There are numerous variations on the basic theme. One variation is that the state-operated or state-aided venture capital organization provides gap financing. It makes up the difference between what a conventional lender will provide and what the firm needs. Perhaps the conventional lender will provide 70 percent of the financing and the firm's principals can provide 10 percent. The venture capital organization might provide the remaining 20 percent in return for a share of the firm. If the firm is successful, the venture capital organization can ultimately "cash out" (sell its equity) and then use this money to capitalize other start-ups.

Typically, venture capital firms have been most common in areas where there is a highly entrepreneurial business culture. The Silicon Valley area is the prototypical example. A question yet to be answered is whether venture capital strategies will be useful in areas where the relative absence of an entrepreneurial business culture is part of the problem. Though venture capital is high-risk lending or investment, it differs from the high-risk lending typically seen in neighborhood development programs, minority business programs, or other programs aimed at either disadvantaged areas or disadvantaged groups. The engineer or scientist with an idea but not much of a business track record is not likely to be a person who meets the normal meaning of "disadvantaged," and there is no geographic targeting intent. The intent is not to help those who need help most, but to spot and nurture promising long shots.

International marketing efforts are relatively new on the state scene. Some states—for example, New York—sent people abroad or maintained overseas offices in the 1970s, but there has been considerable growth in this area in the 1980s. Both the general growth of world trade and the rapid increase in reverse investment would appear to make this trend inevitable. The permanent office in a major European or Asian city and the visiting delegation, often headed by a governor, are the standard approaches. Overseas advertising in most cases is best done at the state level. It is not reasonable to think that substate units of government, except for a few big cities, will be recognizable to European or Asian businesspeople. The task for the economic developer is to be securely tapped into the state efforts so that leads are not missed and his or her bailiwick is not bypassed when the state people shepherd foreign visitors about.

An important caveat must be noted here. As noted earlier, local economic development is a competitive game, and it produces losers as well as winners. Unfortunately, it can have a beggar-my-neighbor quality. This is nowhere more apparent than in some of the overseas prospecting that is currently taking place. For example, a consortium of local economic development agencies in a state in the Southeast made a practice of sending a delegation to the Hanover Trade Fair in West Germany. At the fair the consortium made contact with a European manufacturer of electrical machinery used in manufacturing. The firm, which had no foothold in the U.S. market, wanted to open a small facility in the United States to do sales, some customizing of equipment, and perhaps some final assembly. Consortium personnel were doing everything possible to facilitate this goal. For example, one part of their effort was providing the firm with free marketing assistance to identify U.S. producers and U.S.-made products with which the European firm could compete. In fact, the consortium actually solicited free assistance from a state university in supplying this information.

In effect, the consortium was using public funds to help a foreign producer break into the U.S. market and displace U.S. producers, all in the name of local economic development. It does not take a great deal of economic sophistication to realize that if a product, most of whose value is produced overseas, displaces a comparable product, most of whose value has been produced in the United States, the net effect on U.S. manufacturing employment is negative. The effect on the southern state in question may be positive, for the displacement of U.S. workers may occur in other states. But from the perspective of national interest, the consortium's actions were clearly counterproductive. Whether the consortium personnel thought through the national implications and decided to proceed regardless, or whether in the push for results they never thought through the "big picture," is not known to this writer.

Another big player in the economic development game—and one that is becoming more and more important—is the university. This may be a state or a large private institution. As the focus in U.S. manufacturing shifts further toward high technology, the importance of personnel who are at the very edge of technology grows relative to more traditional locational factors like labor and transportation costs. In many cases the traditional distinctions between labor, management, and ownership break down. Much of the actual work, particularly in the early stages, may be done by the entrepreneur. And much of the labor force, especially in the start-up period, may be people with doctorates in solid-state physics or molecular biology or others who do not fit the usual image of "labor." The major research university, because of its concentration of talent in science and engineering, is likely to be the focal point for high-technology start-ups. It has long been observed that the two centers for microelectronics, the Route 128 corridor around Boston and Silicon Valley in the San Francisco Bay area, formed largely because of the presence of MIT and Harvard in the case of the former and Stanford University in the case of the latter. In 1983 the author mapped the locations of as many genetic engineering firms as he could find. Three clusters emerged. One was in the Boston area, again the influence of Harvard and MIT. A second was in the San Francisco Bay area, again in part the influence of Stanford. A third major cluster was in Maryland, close to the National Institutes of Health, not a university in name but an organization that has many university-like characteristics.

Not only is the university a source of entrepreneurship and professional talent, but its presence helps the high-technology firm to attract the talent it must have. The young engineer or biochemist is more easily recruited by a firm near a university because he or she can pursue a doctorate there or teach there as an adjunct in the evenings. "Quality of life" issues are widely recognized as important factors in attracting high-tech industry and headquarters operations. For many people, the presence of a university is, in itself, a quality-enhancing factor. In another connection it has recently been noted that university towns have been becoming popular as places for retirement because of the cultural enrichment they provide.

The economic developer obviously cannot bring a university into being. However, for the developer who is fortunate enough to be in proximity to a university, the potential advantages should not be squandered. From the developer's perspective, the university is a very big selling point. It may also be a very powerful marketing tool. The faculty of an engineering school, for example, is likely to have contacts at hundreds of manufacturing firms. If the developer can engage members of that faculty in his or her cause, the entrée to firms could be enormous. From 1982 to 1988 the number of science or research parks in the United States almost tripled.[3] The great majority are associated with universities. Goldstein and Lugar note that the biggest factor in attracting high-technology firms is the presence of similar firms. A major university with strength in science and engineering can supplement or perhaps, in some cases, substitute for the presence of an existing high-technology establishment.

Another state innovation of the 1980s has been the enterprise zone. As of the end of 1988, at least thirty states had enterprise zone programs. Several attempts were made to enact legislation creating a federal enterprise zone program, of which the best known was the Kemp-Garcia bill (Jack Kemp, then an upstate New York Republican, and Robert Garcia, a New York City Democrat). None passed both houses and, as of this writing, there is no federal program. Following the failure of the federal effort, the states moved forward on their own. State programs differ widely in their details and extent. In general, there are criteria based on poverty, unemployment, or growth lag that must be met if an area is to be designated. Within the bounds of the designated area various financial incentives are offered to, in effect, "tip the playing field" so as to induce investment. In most cases, some property tax abatement is offered. Investment tax credits and sales tax credits are also commonly offered. Loan guarantees and employment credits may be offered. The latter are payments from the state for each new worker hired by firms within the area. In effect, the state splits the wage bill with the firm.

Enterprise zones are sufficiently new that one cannot be definitive about them. One theoretical question is whether, if the incentives promote an increase in employment in the zone, this will mean an increase in employment within the larger area, or will simply mean a shifting of jobs within the larger area. If an enterprise zone within a city grows as a result of the financial incentives it provides, does this imply net city growth, or does it simply mean redistribution of employment within the city? If it is the former, it may be worthwhile. If it is the latter, it is simply a financial burden on the city and the state that serves no public purpose. In fact, by pushing

up the tax burden, it is making the city and state in general slightly less attractive to business and industry. A second question is whether, ignoring
the net effects, enterprise zones are effective in increasing employment
within their own boundaries. A definitive answer to this question is not
available, but a study of the experience of Maryland from 1983 to 1987
does not demonstrate that the state's program was effective.[4]

Given both the "zero-sum game" issue and the question of effectiveness,
even judged by the more limited standard of growth within the zone itself,
it is difficult to be enthusiastic about state enterprise zones at this stage of
their history. For the economic developer working at the municipal scale,
setting up an enterprise zone in a part of the municipality would appear to
be a fairly low-priority item. The situation might be somewhat different for
a county economic developer in a state that permits the entire county to be
designated as an enterprise zone. The enterprise zone probably has more to
commend itself as a tool for neighborhood or downtown revitalization, a
subject not covered in this book.

NOTES

1. For an account of the efforts of Tennessee and of several other states, see *The
New Economic Role of the States*, R. Scott Fosler, ed., Oxford University Press, New
York, 1988.

2. "The Giveaway Game Continues," Robert Guskind, *Planning*, February 1990,
pp 4–8. See also "State Incentive Packages and the Industrial Location Decision," H.
Brinton Milward and Heidi Hosbach Newman, *Economic Development Quarterly*,
August 1989, pp. 203–22.

3. Harvey A. Goldstein and Michael I. Lugar, "The Potential of Science/
Research Parks as a Regional Development Stimulus," Department of City and Regional Planning, University of North Carolina, Chapel Hill, May 1988.

4. *Enterprise Zones: Lessons from the Maryland Experience*, General Accounting
Office, Washington, D.C., 1988. The report was prepared at the request of Kemp
and Garcia with a view to providing background information for possible future
federal legislation.

6

What Does and Does Not Work

This chapter is based in large measure on a February 1989 survey of the directors of local economic development agencies.[1] The survey contained questions about what they regarded as the most important function of their agency, what activities consumed the largest amounts of their time, what activities they found most and least productive, and what programs they found most and least useful. The information gained from the survey is supplemented by the author's experience and by references to the economic development literature.

VIEWING THE PROBLEM

From the economic developer's perspective, several major facts stand out. First, there are many more communities looking for significant firms than there are firms looking for new locations. Footloose manufacturing is still the economic developer's number-one target. In 1982, the last year for which a count has been published, there were about 34,000 manufacturing firms in the United States with 100 or more employees.[2] Not all of these were footloose. The manufacturer of cement or bricks sells to a local market, and the costs of transporting a low-value-per-pound product tie the firm to that market. For evident reasons, a firm that bakes bread or prints a daily newspaper cannot locate far from its customers. Of those manufacturers who are footloose, only a small percentage will need new or expanded facilities in any given year. Of that minority, most will satisfy their space needs by expansion in place. The percentage of all manufacturers who will branch or relocate to a new community will be relatively small. Perhaps among the 34,000 there will be a few hundred intercommunity moves in a given year. Clearly, there are many more fishermen than fish in this situation.

Most of the big factors influencing location decisions are beyond the control of the economic developer. He or she cannot do much about market access, wage rates, and labor force quality. Climate, topography, and regional infrastructure are beyond the economic developer's control. Quality-of-life issues ranging from school quality and public safety to recreational and cultural facilities are largely beyond the control of the economic developer.

What, then, does the economic developer have to work with? First, he or she has information. Obtaining all of the necessary information upon which to base a location decision can be an expensive and time-consuming proposition. Producing and disseminating information is thus one tool of the economic developer. The cost and difficulty for the firm of collecting and analyzing the data necessary to make a good location choice should not be underestimated. Consider, for example, a manufacturer of a relatively simple product, say, electric fans, who sells to a national market. The firm has decided to open a branch somewhere in the southeastern United States. There are at least several hundred counties that might be suitable. The number of municipalities is still larger. The number of potential sites on which to build is still greater. Or perhaps the firm should not build, but should move into an existing building and either purchase or rent. That expands the range of options still further. Among the items the firm will wish to consider are wage rates, labor force quality, labor force availability, property taxes, sales taxes, corporate income taxes, business inventory taxes, personal income taxes, utility costs, land costs, construction costs, heating costs, building codes, land-use controls, environmental regulations, transport costs, housing costs, the quality of public services, and quality-of-life issues such as public education, public safety, and recreational facilities.

Municipalities can attract businesses by subsidization. But several caveats are necessary here. Numerous studies, both recent and not, have demonstrated that presence or absence of subsidies is not a major determinant of commercial and industrial location. For some types of activities, such as retailing, personal services, and business services, the location of customers is such an overwhelming consideration that there is often little point in thinking about subsidization.

The best candidate for subsidization is "footloose" industry, which generally means manufacturing facilities selling to national or regional markets. But even here, studies show that subsidization is not a major determinant of location.[3] To understand why, one might briefly consider the mathematics of the matter. Assume a factory is to be built in Middletown. Its cost of construction is $40 a square foot. Middletown's property taxes are fairly high, say 2 percent of full value. That works out to 80 cents per square foot per year. Assume Middletown offers the very generous abatement of 50 percent in perpetuity. That saves the firm 40 cents per square foot per year. Assume, as is typical for light manufacturing, that there are 500 square feet of floor space per worker. Assume also that the average worker's total compensation package is $25,000 per year. Assume that for every dollar of wages and salary the firm spends a dollar on raw materials, electric power, and other inputs.[4] On the basis of the above assumptions the firm spends about $100 per square foot per year. Having assumed both a high level of property taxation and a generous tax abatement, the subsidization comes to 0.4 percent (one part in 250) of operating costs. That is not likely to be decisive.

Another point to be made about subsidization is that similar subsidies are offered by many places. In the late 1970s and 1980s hundreds of cities made use of Urban Development Action Grants (UDAGs). For the local economic developer, getting the grant was a nice plum. But many of his or her competitors were getting similar plums from the same source. The point is that it is difficult to be a winner through subsidization. There is probably more chance of being a loser by failing to subsidize when one's competitors are subsidizing.

Finally, subsidizing has something of a "robbing Peter to pay Paul" character. If one gives tax abatements, one shrinks the tax base. If one gives subsidies, one increases the need for revenues. Either way, one puts upward pressure on tax rates. That makes the community less attractive as an economic location. If the tax abatement or subsidy was decisive, the upward pressure on tax rates may have been worth it. If the firm would have moved in (or stayed) anyway, then the subsidy represents a loss.

But can one not be shrewd enough to offer subsidies and tax abatements only when they will be decisive? Opinions on this point differ. Some authors will suggest that the community carefully cost out the firm's situation and offer just enough subsidy to produce an adequate return for the firm. In the writer's view, this sounds much easier than it is. It is in the interest of the firm to convince the economic developer that the subsidy will be decisive. It is in the interest of the community not to be fooled. The company inevitably has better information about its own situation and its own motivations than the community has about them. The firm thus has a big home court advantage. But beyond that, the question in many cases is one not of adequate return but of maximum return. The community is competing not against a minimum rate of return but against another community. As most practicing economic developers soon learn, many businessmen become highly skilled at using the real or fancied offers from one community to motivate the economic development agencies of other communities.

If the subsidy comes from a higher level of government, so that it is essentially costless to the municipality, then the community need not worry overly about whether the subsidy is decisive or is just a windfall. And, in truth, that was one reason for the popularity of Industrial Revenue Bonds (IRBs). It was widely understood that many of them were windfalls; but the fact was that the subsidy, in the form of a tax expenditure, came from the federal government, and even transaction costs such as bond counsel fees could be bonded in and "taken off the top." However, the issuance of IRBs for all but a very limited range of purposes ceased as of December 31, 1989. UDAG grants, which did not require a local match, have effectively come to an end. In short, subsidies that are costless to the municipality are getting rarer.

The local economic developer can play an ombudsman role in which, from the businessman's point of view, government can be converted from enemy to friend. Many businessmen take the matter of "business climate" very seriously. Cutting through red tape and accelerating matters such as the issuance of permits can deliver important cost savings, particularly during periods of high interest rates. Thus, for reasons of both perception and hard cash, the ombudsman role can be important.

Finally, government can play an entrepreneurial role by direct provision of sites and structures. How useful this role is depends upon whether site availability is limiting growth.

SURVEY RESULTS

Table 6.1 shows the opinions of the directors of economic development agencies on the issue of what is the most important agency function. The developers were asked to respond to the choices listed in the table. The emphasis on the information function is clear. There is also a moderate emphasis on grants and financing. The "joint ventures" item was included because in the last several years there has been much discussion of public/private partnerships. The response to it was surprisingly weak. The response to grant applications was also weak, for reasons to be discussed subsequently.

Table 6.1
Economic Developers' Opinions of the Most Important Function of Their Agency

Functions	Percent of responses
Publicizing the area and Providing Information	65
Providing sites	23
Financing	23
Joint ventures	2
Obtaining grants	6
Other	11

Notes: The question was phrased "What would you say is the most important function of your agency?" The choices given were those shown in the table. The numbers add to more than 100 percent because approximately one-fifth of the respondents checked more than one item.

Table 6.2
The Single Activity on Which Economic Development Agencies Spend Most Time

Activity	Percentages of respondents
Sales (Public relations, advertising, provision of data and response to inquiries)	42
Outreach to existing firms	32
Planning and research	8
Site and project development and operations	6
Financing	6
Applications for grants	4
Other	6

Notes: This table and Table 6.3 are derived from the same question. Respondents were asked to use their own words to indicate, in descending order, the five items on which agencies spend the most time. The responses were then grouped by the author. This table indicates the percent of respondents who listed each of the above activities as the number-one time consumer. In the small number of cases where "administration" was listed as number one, the number-two item was substituted. This adjustment was made on the grounds that all agencies must spend time on administration and that it is, in effect, overhead to be spread across all specific activities.

Tables 6.2 and 6.3 summarize how development directors and their staffs allocate their time. Here, developers were asked to respond in their own words; the replies were then grouped by the writer. Table 6.2 lists responses to the question of which single item absorbs the most time, and Table 6.3 lists the five most time-consuming items. The results are generally consistent with Table 6.1. The big items in both tables are the sales (information) function and the outreach to existing industry. The planning, financing, and entrepreneurial functions absorb substantially less time.

Table 6.4 indicates developers' opinions about most and least productive uses of their time. Again, respondents were asked to use their own words, and the replies were grouped by the writer. In the "most productive" column note the large number of responses in the "Sales" and "Outreach" categories. There are a modest number of responses in the "Dealmaking, financing . . ." category and quite small numbers in the other categories. In the least productive column note the large number of responses in the "Grant applications . . ." and "Events and meetings . . ." categories.

These responses, in general, are consistent with those shown in the previous tables. The large number of positive responses to the information function seems readily explained by the fact that the market for business locations is so imperfect with regard to information. For a large firm with a separate corporate planning function, one or more people might be

Table 6.3

Percentages of Respondents Naming Various Activities Among the Top Five Consumers of Time

Activity	Percentages of Respondents
Sales (Public relations, advertising, provision of data and response to inquiries)	80
Outreach to existing firms	70
Planning and research	59
Applications for grants	30
Site and project development and operation	14
Financing	11
Other	29

Note: Derived in the same manner and from the same data as Table 6.2.

assigned to the task on a full-time basis. Alternatively, a location consultant might be used—with fees ranging from three figures for a few hours of conference time at the consultant's office to six figures for a major study. For a small firm neither of these options may be very satisfactory. The firm is not likely to have a corporate planning department, and management is likely to be fully occupied with more short-range problems. The consultant's fee, which may seem trivial to a Fortune 500 firm, may loom large to a small firm. Thus the community that makes itself readily visible and comprehensible has a major advantage over an equivalent community that does not. In effect, the community is a product the development agency sells.

The "Sales" category also drew a moderate number of negative responses and these, too, need a word of explanation. Comments on a number of questionnaires suggest that many of the negative responses in this category specifically pertain to the matter of advertising. For reasons discussed in Chapter 9, advertising is basically directed to a distant audience, unlike public relations, which is necessarily directed to a nearby audience. As suggested earlier, most growth is internally generated, and we know that in any given year there are many more communities seeking to bring in firms than there are firms seeking new locations. Thus a large number of advertising campaigns will necessarily come up empty-handed. Advertising is expensive. For example, at this writing a one-page ad, exclusive of the cost of preparing it, in the best-known economic development publication would be in the $4,000 range. Ads in a major newspaper or a major consumer publication such as *Time* or *Newsweek* will be a large multiple of that figure. Even a modest advertising campaign can be very expensive. If it does not pro-

duce an identifiable payoff, it is easy to see why the frustrated agency director may place advertising in the "least productive" column.

Table 6.4
Most and Least Productive Activities of Economic Development Agencies

Activity	Percent of Responses	
	Most productive	Least productive
Sales activities (Advertising, Public relations, providing data, responding to inquiries)	26	10
Outreach to firms now in jurisdiction	26	2
Dealmaking, financing and Assisting new businesses	9	1
Research and Planning	8	1
Networking	6	1
Site and project development	5	0
Grant applications and compliance and reporting to higher levels of government	3	15
Events and meetings	2	14
Promoting tourism and convention business	2	1
Dealing with politics	0	8
Outside prospecting and overseas marketing	1	3
Other	11	12

Notes: Respondents replied in their own words to the questions "Over the last several
years what do you think was the most (least) productive use of your professional
time?" and the replies were grouped by the author. The terms used by the author
in grouping are as close as possible to the language used by the respondents.
Several respondents indicated more than one most or least productive activity, and
many respondents replied to the "most productive" question but left the "least
productive" question blank. Thus the two column totals are not the same. The
"other" category includes a miscellany of replies that were obviously unique or that
could not be readily coupled to a final activity, for example, "attending seminars" or
"installing a computer system."

The other big item in the "most productive" column is outreach. The
number-one reason that manufacturers move is space needs. In the author's experience—and apparently that of the survey respondents as
well—it is easier to encourage expansions than it is to encourage firms to
branch into or relocate into one's community. In general, firms do not like
to move. Moving is expensive and if one moves far, one loses personnel.
Moving interrupts business. While business is interrupted, one risks losing
customers to one's competitors. The economic developer who can in any
way facilitate an expansion in place has a very good chance of keeping the
firm within his or her community.

Then, to be realistic politically, an effective outreach program is good job insurance for the economic developer. He or she builds a constituency within the community both for the agency in general and for himself or herself in particular.

Some of the other items in Table 6.4 merit discussion as well. "Dealmaking, financing, and assisting new businesses" drew some positive responses, but fewer than the author would have expected. For the municipality that takes a strongly entrepreneurial role, dealmaking—for example, signing a lease for a site in the municipal industrial park—is the ultimate goal. But many economic development agencies do not play an entrepreneurial role. Or they may play an entrepreneurial role that is minor relative to the total of such activity. For example, there may be a municipal industrial park but there may also be privately owned industrial parks, or the lion's share of industrial development may occur on scattered, privately owned parcels. The agency may do some dealmaking, but this may be relatively small in comparison with the number of deals put together by the commercial real estate establishment in the community. In any case, the response to the "Dealmaking . . ." question was not trivial, but it was small compared with the first two items on the list. "Site and project development" also did not draw many positive responses, perhaps for similar reasons.

The "Grant applications and compliance, and reporting to higher levels of government" response is interesting. Grant applications and compliance were coupled because so much reporting to higher levels of government is in connection with grants. The percentage of directors who listed grant applications as their "most productive" activity is very small. It is possible that the small figure partially represents the shrinkage of federal grant programs under the Reagan administration, and that had the same question been asked in 1979 instead of 1989, the response would have been larger. However, at this writing, there is little indication that the flow of federal grants for local economic development is likely to increase. The federal budget deficit and the Bush administration's unyielding position on tax increases suggest that, if anything, continued tightness is most likely. One might expect that the states would step in and use their own funds to replace diminished federal funds, but this has not yet happened. One effect of diminished federal transfers to the states has been increased fiscal pressure on the states, which militates against increases in state funding for local economic development.

The large number of "least productive" responses to the grants category merits some notice. About half of those responding in the "least productive" category cited both the time required to do grant applications and the fact that grant applications are a competitive process in which there is always a substantial chance of not being funded. The amount of time that the grant application process can soak up should not be underrated. The other half of the respondents cited having to do grant applications that they knew would not be funded but that they had to do for political reasons. If the grant program is there, the economic developer may have to apply simply to defend against the charge of negligence. "We gave it our best shot but we didn't get it" sounds better than "In my professional judgment the probability of getting it did not justify the amount of effort the application process involved." Having to do things against one's better judgment is one of the prices the economic developer may have to pay for his or her high visibility. The author once spent hundreds of hours of his time going through the entire EDA application process when he was convinced that the chances of success were virtually nil. But someone else within the same government had gone public with statements about the possibility of obtaining EDA grants and thus, politically, there was no choice but to go through the motions.

Another aspect of the grant process to consider is timing. In general, there are long delays and it is often difficult for firms to wait out the application process. This is particularly so if the program is highly competitive, for then uncertainty about the ultimate outcome compounds the delay problem.

The response to the "Events and meetings" question in some ways mirrors the response to the grants question. Some events are clearly worthwhile. Meetings with firms are always to be sought. So, too, are meetings with parties who influence firms or participate in the dealmaking process. For example, very little serious business is consummated without participation of lawyers and bankers. Attending a meeting of the local bar association or bankers' association at which one can say a few words about the operations and plans of one's agency is time well spent. In a large community there are likely to be one or more real estate brokers who specialize in commercial transactions. Time spent meeting with them is clearly worthwhile, for the majority of commercial land purchases and building rentals will be mediated by them. But there are many meetings that are not productive but must be attended for political reasons—again, the price of political visibility and vulnerability. The author was somewhat surprised by the number of respondents who specifically listed meetings with state officials as their least productive activity.

Another response the author found surprising was the very weak showing in the "Outside prospecting and overseas marketing" category. In part the low response to "outside" propsecting may represent the flip side of the axiom that for most places most growth is internally generated. It also may reflect the fact that outside prospecting, like sales calls in distant locations, is time consuming and expensive. Finally, it may indicate that responding to inquiries is a more efficient way of dealing with firms at a distance than is extensive traveling. The weak response to "Overseas marketing" is also surprising. As suggested in another chapter, overseas marketing is probably better done by the state than by the locality in most cases. For reasons noted in Chapter 4, the writer believes that overseas marketing will take on more importance in years to come. But it must be admitted that as of 1989, most local economic developers showed little enthusiasm for it. As suggested in Chapter 4, some of the present state efforts in overseas marketing may have a certain "beggar-my-neighbor" effect when viewed nationally, and probably merit some skepticism and restraint on those grounds as well.

The survey also asked practitioners whether they targeted much in their recruitment efforts. In general, the answer was "no." The commonly used categorization of industry is the Standard Industrial Classification (SIC) system. In this system all economic activity is broken down into a few one-digit codes, such as Manufacturing and Trade. Each of these codes is then broken down into two-digit codes, so that all U.S. economic activity is categorized by about ninety two-digit codes. For example, manufacturing is broken down into twenty two-digit codes, SIC 20 through SIC 39. At the two-digit level the categorizations are quite broad. For example, SIC 37 is transportation equipment, which covers a range from bicycles to space shuttles. Each two-digit code is then subdivided into three- and four-digit codes. For example, SIC 371 is motor vehicles and equipment. Going to four digits, code 3711 is motor vehicle and car bodies, code 3713 is truck and bus bodies, code 3714 is motor vehicle parts and accessories, and so on.

For the economic developer who has a general familiarity with business and industry and who knows his or her community fairly well, it should be possible to reach the two-digit level almost intuitively. Yet as Table 6.5 shows, only 10 percent of development directors indicated that they target beyond the two-digit level. On the surface, it would seem that precise targeting would be a way to achieve maximum efficiency in spending one's advertising and marketing dollars. The conceptual tools for precise targeting are available, and the academic literature contains considerable advice on how to go about it. The question, then, is why so few agencies do serious targeting.

As suggested in connection with outside prospecting, the limited amount of targeting may also be a reflection of the relative importance of locally generated growth versus growth through the recruitment of outside firms. The outreach effort is obviously not subject to targeting. One reaches out to the firms that are now in the community, regardless of what they are and regardless of whether they seem to be the types of firms that, on the basis of objective criteria, ought to be there.

It also may be that there are enough unpredictable elements in the business location decision that targeting cannot be done so effectively as its proponents suggest. The majority of firms with which the economic developer deals are small, closely held corporations. That means that their stock is not public, but is owned by a very small number of principals. The majority of shares may be held by a single individual or, often, by a husband and wife. In effect, there is little of the separation between ownership and manage-

Table 6.5
Degree of Sectoral Targeting Specificity

Level of Specificty	Percentage of respondents
No targeting	22
Targeting at the 1 digit SIC Level	25
Targeting at the 2 digit SIC Level	34
Targeting at the 3 or 4 digit SIC Level	10
Indicated targeting but supplied no specifics	8

Notes: Based on replies to the question "Do you actively recruit firms? (yes) (no). If yes, do you target particular types of firms or particular industries? Please specify." The characterizations in the table are based on the SIC code, but since respondents replied in their own terms rather than SIC terms, some interpretation was necessary. A reply like "corporate headquarters," "manufacturing," or "light manufacturing" would be recorded at the one-digit SIC level. A reply like "metalworking industries" or "food processing" would be recorded at the two-digit SIC level. Anything more specific, such as "medical instruments," would be listed at the three- or four-digit SIC level.
Totals do not add to 100 due to rounding.

ment that there usually is in a very large corporation. Management thus does not have to account to a board of directors or to the stockholders for its decisions. Personal considerations and viewpoints that could not be justified objectively may weigh very heavily in location decisions. Thus issues like personal residential and life-style preferences may influence the decision. So, too, may idiosyncratic (though not necessarily incorrect) business opinions. The author once asked an entrepreneur why, given the energy-intensive nature of die casting, he was thinking of locating a die-casting facility in a municipality within the boundaries of the most expensive major electric utility in the United States. The answer was "I've done business here before, and I like the labor force." Another businessman, who stayed in New York state even though the state of Pennsylvannia had made him a financial offer that the New York community in which he was located would not match, said simply, "I don't know anyone in Pennsylvannia. What would I do there?"

Even with large publicly held corporations, where "bottom line" is the watchword of the day, large personal elements creep into the decision-making process. There is no doubt that one reason so many corporate headquarters in the New York metropolitan area are located in the Westchester/Fairfield area is that the corporate people who make the location decisions like to live there.

The writer once was visited in his office by the director of the U.S. branch of a large European corporation seeking to relocate its headquarters. The official asked extensive questions about finding a sheltered workshop in which his handicapped child might enroll. Though this consideration would never appear in a report to his superiors in Europe, it was obvious that he intended to bend the decision toward a personal need that was important to him.

Perhaps still another factor that causes economic developers to do less targeting than might be expected is inherent in the nature of public relations. As will be argued in Chapter 9, public relations efforts often give a much bigger "bang for the buck" than do advertising efforts. But, by its very nature, public relations cannot be targeted nearly so precisely as advertising. One sends out a press release and it is used by anyone who chooses to use it, in whatever manner he or she chooses to use it. The resulting inquiries and contacts cannot be predicted in advance.

Finally, the small size of most economic development agencies is probably a factor. Staff may be sufficiently occupied with outreach and responding to inquiries that it is not possible to find the uninterrupted time to design and implement a targeted recruiting program.

In any case, precise targeting informed by the analytical tools of location theory and financial analysis is not in widespread use by practitioners, even though it is widely recommended by many who write on economic development. A number of economic developers believe in it more than they practice it. In reply to the question of whether his agency targeted, one economic developer replied, "Theoretically, yes; practically, no."

Table 6.6 shows responses to questions about the usefulness of various forms of financial assistance available from the federal, state, and local governments. One caveat about the data in the table deserves mention. Some forms of assistance are available almost everywhere, while others, such as EDA and UDAG grants, are available only in some areas. Thus a large number in the "least useful or no experience" column may reflect eligibility limits and not be a comment on program quality. Also, the table reflects experience over a number of years, and the funding scene has changed substantially in the last several years.

By far the most popular program in the table is IRBs. The reasons for their popularity are clear. In general, their issuance was not competitive and required no application to the federal government. The federal government was informed of the issuance of the bond(s) after the fact through the filing of a document referred to as a "certificate of election." This simply indicated that the bond issuer was electing to issue the bond pursuant to certain provisions of the IRS code pertaining to exempt small issues. At this writing, the issuance of IRBs is of more historical than practical interest. However, to the extent that the popularity of IRBs was largely a function of their noncompetitive nature and relative freedom from bureaucratic procedures, there may be a lesson regarding the desirable attributes of a funding program.

At the state level there is a relatively strong endorsement of revolving loan funds. It seems likely that the relative simplicity of such programs and the absence of need for consultation with higher levels of government may account for part of their high rating.

Many "other" replies were provided by the economic developers surveyed. A number listed state-level infrastructure grants as being most helpful. Several listed state loan programs that did not fit any of the categories in the questionnaire. Only one economic developer listed manpower training funds as being "most useful." In view of the fact that a number of states, particularly in the South, offer manpower training that is specifically keyed to firm needs—as distinct from applicant need, as was the case with the Comprehensive Employment and Training Act—this is a somewhat surprising result. One would expect such training to be a significant inducement, but the survey did not bear this out.[5]

Table 6.6
Most and Least Useful Programs

Program	Percent of Responses		
	Most useful	Somewhat useful	Least Useful or no experience
Federal			
Community Development Block Grant	40	48	13
Urban Development Action Grants	24	33	40
Economic Development Administration	36	25	38
Small Business Administration	29	50	19
Industrial Revenue Bonds	73	18	10
State and local			
Investment tax credits	25	36	38
Mortgage guarantees	16	33	46
Interest rate reductions	44	29	26
Loan guarantees	39	37	24
Enterprise zones	23	36	35
Revolving loan funds	48	33	19
Venture capital funds	16	41	35
Small Business Investment Corporations	6	34	51

Note: Figures may not add to 100 across rows due to rounding or incomplete filling out by respondents.

A CONCLUDING NOTE

If one were to distill some practical advice from all of the above, what would it be? First, recognize that for most agencies, local economic development is largely a selling operation. It is not the type of selling that relies upon the manipulation of images or emotional appeal, as is much selling of consumer products. Rather, it is a very factual and data-intensive selling process. But it is still selling. Clearly, then, establishing a database and making the agency widely known should be high-priority items.

Outreach to the existing economic base is crucial. As noted, the major share of growth in most communities is locally generated. Then, too, local firms can be reached at a small fraction of the per firm cost of distant firms.

The two items above should be given first priority by most agencies. If it is politically feasible, significant effort should not be devoted to other activities until these two are well in hand.

Most agencies do pursue grant monies, but it is well to think about the odds and the time costs before deciding to go after a particular grant. For example, at this writing the Economic Development Administration (EDA) is funded at slightly under $200 million. Areas containing about 90 percent of the U.S. population are eligible for EDA funding. That works out to perhaps 75 cents per capita. The possibility of obtaining a grant is attractive. And, as Table 6.6 indicates, a substantial number of economic developers apparently think well of their experience with EDA. But before deciding to pursue EDA funding, some careful thought should be given to the time required and the probability of success, for effort devoted to that purpose is inevitably effort taken from something else. UDAG, as noted, appears to be at an end. In the 1989 fiscal year it operated on $50 million in "recaptured" funds. UDAG grants, too, are attractive, and in the past hundreds of municipalities have benefited from them. But with a $50 million "pot" the odds in 1989 were very long indeed. In general, a policy of applying for every grant for which one is technically eligible is not a cost-effective strategy.

Should your agency play an entrepreneurial role, perhaps through a publicly developed industrial park or a shell building? There is no question that such a role is politically attractive. It conveys a picture of dynamism, of doing something concrete, of not just printing brochures, issuing press releases, or giving speeches to Rotary clubs. But, politics aside, the question is whether it is necessary. Can it be fairly said that absence of sites or buildings is the limiting factor in community growth? Does the community have, or does it not have, commercial real estate firms that are competent to show sites and put together deals? Would a community-owned facility stand alone, or would it compete with existing privately owned industrial and commercial sites? How much vacant industrial and commercial land and floor space is there in the area, and what has been its rate of absorption in recent years? Is the failure of the community to attract new firms due to the price of land or structures being a bit too high, or are there more fundamental reasons? When one has the answers to these and similar questions, one can think effectively about whether an entrepreneurial role makes sense.

NOTES

1. The questionnaire was mailed to 320 randomly chosen development agency directors listed in the 1989 Economic Development Directory in the October 1988 issue of *Area Development*. The survey excluded chambers of commerce, consultants, and specialized organizations such as port authorities and free trade zones. The usable response rate was approximately 35 percent.

2. *Statistical Abstract of the United States*, 108th edition, Bureau of the Census, U.S. Department of Commerce, Washington, D.C., 1988, table 1241. For further statistics on manufacturing, see either *Census of Manufacturing*, published by the Bureau of the Census in years ending in 2 and 7, or the *Annual Survey of Manufacturing*, also published by the Bureau of the Census.

3. There is a very large literature on this subject. See Dennis S. Tosh et al., "Industrial Site Selection Criteria: Are Economic Developers, Manufacturers and Industrial Real Estate Brokers Operating on the Same Wavelength," *Economic Development Review*, Fall 1988, pp. 62–67; and Gordon D. Hack, "Location Trends: 1958–88," *Area Development*, October 1988, p. 12. See also Roger W. Schmenner, *Making Business Location Decisions*, Prentice-Hall, Englewood Cliffs, N.J., 1982; Daryll A. Hellman et al., *State Financial Incentives to Industry*, Lexington Books D.C. Heath, Lexington, Mass., 1976. For a good review of older literature, see George A. Reigeluth and Harold Wolman, "The Determinants and Implications of Communities' Changing Competitive Advantage: A Review of Literature," Urban Institute, Washington, D.C., 1979 (working paper no. 1264–03).

4. This is a very casual estimate based on the fact that at present, value added by manufacturing in the United States is in the $1 trillion range and the total value of shipments by U.S. manufacturing firms is in the $2 trillion range. Detailed statistics on value added and value of shipments by industry can be found in the *Annual Survey of Manufacturing*.

5. The Comprehensive Employment and Training Act, which was targeted to the disadvantaged, was ended in 1983 and replaced by the Jobs Training and Partnership Act (JTPA), jointly introduced by Senators Edward Kennedy and Dan Quayle. The JTPA lacks the public-sector employment components of CETA and is funded at much lower levels than was CETA in its heyday. JTPA is discussed in Ch. 11.

7

Reasonable Expectations

Having sketched the economic development scene, some words on what reasonable expectations a community and new economic development agency might hold seem appropriate. A community cannot make a reasoned decision on whether an economic development program is worthwhile if it has no notion of what the results may be. Nor can it judge an economic development agency and its personnel if it doesn't have some sense of what to expect. Educating the body politic about reasonable expectations is thus time well spent for the economic developer.

The first thing for the community to realize is how competitive the local economic development scene is. As noted in connection with footloose manufacturing, the number of firms of significant size that will relocate in one year is a tiny fraction of the number of local economic development programs in the United States. It is also important to realize that many of the determinants of economic growth are beyond community control. Very often the goal is seen as bringing in new industry. The economic developer is the fisherman who will bring home a huge fish upon which all can dine happily. But the truth, as noted before, is that most agencies achieve most of their success from nurturing the economic base they have. The economic development agency, if events go reasonably well, is much more likely to have small successes—expansions facilitated and departures forestalled— than it is to have spectacular achievements like a new Fortune 500 corporate headquarters.

When there is a success, whether large or small, and whether home-grown or of outside origin, it may be difficult to tell exactly how much credit should go to the community's economic development agency. When a firm moves in or expands in place, the development agency, the local commercial real estate community, the banking community, the Public Works Department, the Planning Department, the chamber of commerce, and the office of the mayor or the county executive or the city manager may all have a hand in the process. If grants, loans, bonds, tax abatements, or the like were offered, they may or may not have been decisive. The firm that wants them will, of course, insist that the deal could not have been swung without them. But only the firm really knows for certain.

It is important for a community to understand that economic development is not predictable. As in fishing, one cannot say what one will catch or when one will catch it. One can say that, most of the time, the location decision is not made quickly. The biggest single reason for relocating is that the firm outgrows its facility. Usually the event can be forecast several years in advance. That gives the firm plenty of time to evaluate all the possibilities: expansion in place, branching, relocating, or outsourcing. Occasionally a firm may have to find new space quickly, perhaps because of a sudden increase in demand or a catastrophic event like a fire. But such haste is clearly the exception. Though one may think of the private sector as quick and decisive and the public sector as more sluggish, it is very often the case that the public-sector people move more quickly. The firm's representatives appear and ask for some information. The development agency personnel drop everything to put together a package as quickly as possible. Then nothing is heard from the firm for two months. Agency personnel wonder what has happened and whether, perhaps, they did not do enough. But the firm is just proceeding rationally. Its corporate planning people foresaw the need for new space three years ahead of the time it will actually be needed, and they are conducting their search at a measured and sensible pace. And, aside from that, if they are going to ask this community for a tax concession or some other "freebie," there is no sense in acting overeager. It is much better to act as if there are many other equally good locations and as if this community will be very fortunate even to make their short list.

Many local economic development programs are done for property tax reasons. It is good to be realistic about the tax effects of a successful program, which can vary enormously. If new economic development simply scales up the community, the effects on the tax rate may be minuscule. Like multiplying an equation by a constant, the effect may simply be to scale up both the cost and the revenue side equally. In special circumstances discussed in Chapter 12, economic development programs may yield substantial property tax decreases, but these circumstances are more the exception than the rule. A useful and simple exercise is to hypothesize how much in the way of new ratables a successful effort might bring in and then take that figure as a percent of the present real property tax base. Then assume no new costs whatsoever. That provides an absolute upper limit on the percentage reduction in property taxes. Then lay that figure off against the property tax burden on the median house to get an absolute dollar figure. The results of this simple exercise can be quite sobering.

Labor market effects of economic development are often not as dramatic as a naïve calculation might suggest. As discussed in Chapter 12, migration tends to dilute the effect on the unemployed population. The community may be surprised to find that though a new plant employing 100 workers has opened, only a dozen workers have been taken off the unemployment rolls. Multiplier effects from local economic development can vary enormously, a point also discussed in Chapter 12. It should not be automatically assumed that each job in a new facility will provide another two jobs or so in ancillary activity. Much of the multiplier effect may show up outside the community borders. And some of the new jobs may simply constitute displacement—jobs in the new shopping center replacing jobs in the existing retailing district.

Finally, from the community perspective, there should be an understanding that economic development programs may promote some conflict within the community, most often over traffic, loss of open space, or land-use planning considerations. In the writer's observation, conflict may be most severe in a community with a large upper-middle-class population that has a strong environmental commitment and that may not earn its living in the community. There is also regional variation. Environmentally based opposition to economic growth is likely to be stronger in New England or the Pacific Northwest than in the South.

From the economic developer's point of view, ensuring that the community has a realistic view of what can and cannot be done makes for a better relationship between development agency and the body politic. It makes it possible to design a program for maximum cost effectiveness. And it is good job insurance. If the unpredictability and slowness of the economic development process is explained to the community before the economic developer begins to work, he or she will be appreciated for being forthright. If the same things are said a year or two into the process, they will seem like excuses. If the community has unrealistic expectations because of glowing pictures painted by the economic developer, then he or she is standing in a deep hole of his or her own digging and there is not much useful advice to be given except to keep his or her résumé up to date.

The median agency in the writer's survey noted earlier had a full-time staff of three or four people (the average size was about six because of the effect of a limited number of quite large agencies). A staff of three or four people cannot do everything, so an important matter of agency policy is to decide what it will concentrate on and what it will leave to others. Ideally, this should be decided on a cost-effectiveness basis, and the body politic should buy into the understanding. That gives the agency some protection against recriminations beginning with "Why didn't you . . . ?" If that kind of understanding cannot be reached, then a certain amount of agency time is likely to spent on politically necessary but essentially useless activity.

For the essential core of activity for the average agency, the writer would nominate some of the activities suggested by the survey findings noted in Chapter 6. These items would include developing and maintaining a solid database, a continuous outreach program to the existing business community, and a public relations program that assures agency visibility. The latter, discussed in detail in Chapter 8, basically means publicizing activities and concrete accomplishments through press releases, interviews, articles, and the like. It means a certain amount of public speaking to groups like Rotary, Kiwanis, and the local bar association. It also means making oneself known in the business and government communities, a process that a number of respondents identified as "networking."

If the body politic has reasonable expectations and does not expect all things from its development agency, grants should be pursued judiciously. Effort will be put in only when pursuing the grant seems cost effective.

As indicated before, the writer would urge caution about plunging into entrepreneurial activities. If there is a real void in private sector activity, they may be necessary. It is not a good idea to pursue them simply because they look like the dynamic, activist thing to do.

Another item to be cautious about is competition with the real estate industry. Real estate brokers should be the economic developer's allies. They basically have the same interests. Unless the brokerage industry is absent or incompetent, listing and showing sites should be left to brokers. Since it is their full-time activity, they are likely to be better at it. Rather than competing with them, it is better to cooperate by supplying data, providing advice on funding programs, and the like.

8

Public Relations, Advertising, and Marketing

As the other chapters in this book have suggested, selling is the single most important activity of most economic developers. This chapter, though it occupies only a small percent of the pages in this book, is really the central chapter. The "selling" that an economic development agency does is technical selling. The industrial equivalent is sales engineering. Nobody chooses an industrial site or rents space in a commercial building on a whim. If the community is not right for the firm, the economic developer is not going to sell the firm on that community. On the other hand, one can lose a firm that is right for one's community because the firm does not know about the community.

The chapter is divided into five sections:

1. Public relations
2. Advertising
3. Outreach
4. Direct selling
5. The Database.

PUBLIC RELATIONS

By "public relations" is meant all those activities, other than paid advertising, which increase the visibility of the agency and the municipality. The distinction between advertising and public relations is that advertising involves paying for space (or air time) and public relations does not. The goals are very much the same.

Public relations is generally short range. The local press will regard what your agency does as news and give you coverage. But the press in distant places will not. A fundamental fact about the local press is that it is hungry for news. A daily newspaper or a weekly business paper has much "white space" to be filled. It wants copy just as much as you want coverage. A great deal of what appears as news was not ferreted out by a reporter, but came to the newspaper as a press release. The role of the reporter is often to call back and verify or clarify. Occasionally, if the story is big enough or interesting enough, the reporter may visit in person.

Material that appears in the press from public relations activity is often much more effective than an equivalent amount of space devoted to advertising. From a very early age most of us learn to distinguish between the program and the commercial and between the article and the ad. We tend to discount advertising because we know it is fundamentally self-serving. Public relations material, in contrast, comes under the radar screen of disbelief. One does not read an article in the business section and think "I'll bet that article is just a lightly edited press release," even though much business news is exactly that. The handiwork of the PR man or woman comes to us as news and we tend to accept it as news. And it really is news. If a press release is all fluff and no substance, a good paper will not use it. And, of course, one function of the editor is to remove the fluff and retain the substance.

A press release is basically a news story written by the party who would like the press coverage. It has a headline and sometimes a subhead. It then contains a news story. Typically the story is written in the "inverted pyramid" style. The first sentence or two contains the who, what, why, where, and when of the story. Subsequent paragraphs fill in the details. It is written so that if it is cut at any point, the material above that point still makes sense on its own. If the newspaper decides to print only the first paragraph and discard the rest of the release, the essentials of the story still have gotten through.

Several basic points about press releases need to be made. The first is to be absolutely truthful. If you are not, you will lose credibility and subsequent releases will go directly into the wastepaper basket. Since you will have repeated dealings with the same editors, be reliable. Do not complain about how your press release was treated. There is wisdom in the old aphorism "Never argue with someone who buys ink by the barrel." A point to remember is that once you have sent out a press release, you no longer have any control. Do not ask an editor or reporter if you can see what will be written before it appears. This will be taken as an affront to the editor's or reporter's integrity and will be refused. Do not try to couple advertising and news coverage by suggesting that if news coverage is given, advertising orders will be forthcoming. No editor with journalistic integrity will tolerate that. Any reputable publication regards advertising and editorial as separate operations.

What constitutes a publicizable action? Almost anything that the agency does. The setting up of the agency is a publicizable event. Appointment of members to its board is publicizable. If the agency prints a map or a brochure, that is publicizable. An example is shown below.

Development Agency Releases Traffic Map

The East Nowhere Economic Development Agency has produced a map showing traffic volumes on main and secondary roads throughout the county. According to James Smith, agency director, "We think East Nowhere has considerable potential for retailing development and we know that traffic volumes are of major interest to retailers." The map was developed from State Highway Department data by development agency personnel. It is the latest in a series of publications by the East Nowhere Economic Development Agency. Earlier items include . . . . Copies of the map or other items may be obtained by writing or calling . . . .

The press release should be accompanied by a copy of the map. A cover letter is not required. Given that the newspaper will treat this as a very minor news item, a short release, as above, is adequate. The press coverage will serve two functions. The article may come to the notice of a firm that will consider locating in the area. But even if it does not, it informs firms and the public that the agency exists and is a source of information and assistance.

Even what seem like trivial actions by agency personnel may be publicizable. If you give a talk at the Rotary club on what East Nowhere is doing about economic development, that is publicizable. A brief press release might be worded as follows:

James Smith, director of the East Nowhere Economic Development Agency, will address the East Nowhere Rotary Club on "Financing New Industry" this Thursday at noon at Alfredo's Steak House. The agency, founded last April, is now beginning a program to . . . .

It will not get much press coverage, but if only the first sentence is printed, it will inform people that the agency exists, what its purpose is, and who its head is.

Any concrete accomplishment by the agency, of course, should be publicized. Below is a copy of a press release from the Westchester County, New York, economic development agency at the time it was run by the writer. The release is short and factual. Quite evidently it did not take very long to write. The story got coverage in the *New York Times* and a number of other papers. The *Times*, which has a large staff and takes pride in its thoroughness, called back to verify and clarify the story. Other papers simply picked it up and used it, sometimes with substantial editing and sometimes more or less as written. The equivalent amount of advertising space would have cost many thousands of dollars. And, as suggested earlier, the articles were probably more effective than advertising.

For Information Contact: FOR IMMEDIATE RELEASE
(Contact name)
(phone number)
$1 MILLION WCIDA FINANCING BRINGS BELGIAN FIRM TO
WESTCHESTER

As a result of a joint effort of the Westchester County Industrial Development Agency (WCIDA) and the New York State Department of Commerce, WCIDA's second financing, a $1 million bond issue, has been completed. This will enable Ordibel, Inc., the American division of a Belgian company, to expand its U.S. operations to a 40,000 square foot building in Westchester. Aided by tax-exempt financing provided through the WCIDA, Ordibel, a manufacturer of collators and sorters, is moving into a headquarters building at 543 Tarrytown Road, Greenburgh. Ordibel was brought to the WCIDA by William S. Junor, ombudsman of the New York State Department of Commerce.

"We're quite excited that Ordibel will be locating in Westchester," commented County Executive Alfred B. DelBello, "and we are additionally pleased to see continuing cooperation among the various government agencies in the field of economic development. The Ordibel facility in Greenburgh will mean about 100 new jobs for the county, most of them blue-collar. The move of Ordibel, a Belgian company, is particularly gratifying since it demonstrates once again the desirability of Westchester as the location for international corporations."

The bond-purchase arrangements added to the international flavor. Approximately half the bonds were bought by the National Bank of Westchester. The balance of the bonds were purchased by a group of private investors, both foreign and American, and guaranteed by Societe du Belgique, a Belgian bank. The $1 million of bonds were issued for a 10-year term at a rate of 7.25%, resulting in considerable debt service savings for the company.

Anthony C. Clarkson, president of Ordibel, said that the purchase of the Greenburgh building was greatly enhanced by attractive WCIDA financing. He also remarked, "Ordibel was able to secure just the right building for our American headquarters, a building which permits us to establish fabricating and assembling functions as well as general offices. Locating in Westchester allows us to remain close to our most vital commercial and market areas." Mr. Clarkson said that Ordibel had investigated other sites in Illinois, Georgia, New Jersey, and Connecticut before choosing Westchester.

What about quotes in the press release? The quote in a press release does not literally mean the person being quoted spontaneously uttered those very words. It means that the person in question approved the release before it was sent out, thus agreeing to be quoted in that manner.

To whom should press releases be sent? The agency should maintain a standard press release mailing list. This would normally include local newspapers, regional newspapers, business publications, and any groups that publish newsletters which might cover economic development stories. The press release will carry a release date. Care should be taken that it arrives early enough to be used by the release date. A press release that arrives after the release date is not likely to be used because, having been run by other publications, it is no longer news. For larger stories, the agency may consider giving the material to a particular publication as an exclusive. One is likely to get better coverage in the selected publication, but one loses all other coverage. For most items, a mailing to the standard list is adequate.

Apart from the press release, there are many other ways to approach the press. One way is to offer to write a piece for publication. The general press can sometimes be gotten into this way, and the business press very often can be. Call the editor and ask if he or she would be interested in a piece along the lines of. . . . Alternatively, one can send the editor a letter that describes the proposed article in a few sentences and follow the letter with a phone call. In general, it is not wise to spend hours writing a piece without some expression of editorial interest.

The copy below is the beginning of an article by the author that appeared in the Westchester/Rockland supplement of the Sunday *New York Times* under the heading "What the County Is Doing to Keep Economically Healthy." The writer simply called the editor and asked if she would be interested in an article discussing the county's economic development program. The article occupied about half a page and would have cost many thousands of dollars as advertising. The cost for the author's agency was a day or two of the author's time.

Question: What does Westchester County have in common with Atlanta, Houston, Phoenix, and Sedalia, Mo.? Answer: Westchester, like the others, is wooing potential business and pursuing an active economic development policy.

Do we really have to do this? After all, isn't Westchester one of the nation's most affluent counties and aren't we still a symbol of suburban affluence?

Yes, on the average, we are still one of the nation's wealthiest counties. And we haven't suffered the economic and fiscal crises that New York City has gone through. Westchester bonds are still triple A.

But averages and images don't tell the whole story. Perhaps you're a blue-collar worker out of work because your employer has left the county; a homeowner groaning under a massive property-tax increase because the tax base of your town has stopped growing; a young college graduate looking for an entry-level job in a highly competitive labor market. Or . . . .

The business press is generally easier to get into than the general press. Some business journals are primarily scissors-and-paste operations. A visitor to the office of the publication will be startled by how small the staff is. One may wonder how so few people can put out so much copy each week. The press release and the contributed article are the answer. And, of course, the business press is exactly where one wants to be. It goes to those people you most want to reach. The approach is as above. Call and ask if the publication would like a piece on. . . . The following is the beginning of an article by the writer that appeared in a local business journal. The article, under the headline "Growth Incentives Available for Builders and Businessmen," ran about twenty-five column inches and was, in effect, an ad for the writer's agency.

Builders and developers in Westchester County have a wide range of development financing and tax abatement programs available to them.

Development financing programs provide money for construction and renovation at below market rates, and mortgage guarantees can make the difference for projects which might not be possible with purely conventional financing. Tax abatement programs are available both to reduce property tax liability and corporate income tax liability.

Construction Financing

Tax exempt financing in the form of industrial revenue bonds is available . . . .

Another way to approach the local press is the invited article. Again, the best approach is to call the editor and ask if he or she would be interested in doing an article on. . . . For example, if the city or county has just set up an economic development agency, would there be interest in doing an article on the agency's goals and personnel? If the agency has just completed a deal, or if a new firm has just moved in, or if an old firm has just completed an expansion, the agency might ask whether the paper would be interested in doing an article on it. Most firms like publicity and will be pleased to cooperate. If the answer is "yes," then arrangements will be made and a reporter (perhaps also a photographer) will show up at the appointed time.

Another aspect of public relations is public speaking. In fact, this is what people in marketing sometimes refer to as a "twofer." The speaking engagement spreads your message directly, and the fact that you will speak is itself publicizable. If nobody shows up for the speech, you will still get some mileage out of the press release. But how does one get invited to speak? The easiest way is to call and ask, or write a brief letter offering your services. Many groups have a continuing need for speakers. For example, Rotary clubs generally meet weekly. A typical format is to have lunch or dinner and a speaker who talks for perhaps twenty minutes, beginning after the main course. Very often the Rotary clubs in an area will have a program chairman. One call or letter to the program chairman may get you on numerous clubs' calendars. The same talk, perhaps customized slightly for the particular group, can be given repeatedly. Most Rotary members are business people and thus are a good audience to reach. Comparable comments can be made about organizations like Lions or Kiwanis. The talk can be quite straightforward. Tell them what your agency does and why it is doing it. It is a good idea to leave people with something that will remind them of the talk. Thus you might take copies of an agency brochure to hand out. In fact, when developing the database, you might consider printing one general flyer, in a narrow format that fits into the breast pocket of a suit jacket, to give out at such occasions.

The League of Women Voters is another organization that uses speakers, and its civic-minded membership is likely to be interested in local economic development issues. One might try to soften future opposition by approaching conservationist or environmental organizations with an offer to talk on reconciling the needs of economic growth and environmental quality.

Two other groups to reach are lawyers and bankers, for little significant business activity takes place without them. Find out if there is a local bar association and a bankers' association, and offer yourself or a member of your staff as a speaker. If the area is large enough to have a number of firms that handle commercial real estate, find out if they have an organization or if they meet periodically, and offer to address them. Beyond addressing bankers, lawyers, and brokers in a formal manner, it is worthwhile to meet with them on a one-to-one basis. The most direct way to do this is to call and ask, in effect, "May I meet with you and tell you something about our agency?" Such meetings make your agency known, and they inform you about what is happening in the business community.

It is important to have people who are comfortable with the contact and speaking part of the operation. Many people who exhibit no diffidence in ordinary social situations may find public speaking and calling up strangers to be intimidating. Therefore, they may find all sorts of reasons to put off these tasks. This is a point to be considered when hiring.

ADVERTISING

One advertises to reach firms that are beyond the reach of public relations activity. It is generally not cost effective to advertise locally. Local firms and businessmen can be reached far more effectively by public relations techniques such as those described above. Before discussing the mechanics of advertising, we should consider the question of whether to advertise at all. Advertising by itself, like public relations by itself, will not cause anyone to invest in your community. All it does is open a dialogue. The ad brings an inquiry and the agency responds to that inquiry. A more or less standard way to respond to an inquiry from an ad is to send a brochure and a covering letter. This is followed a week or two later with a "Did you receive our brochure?" phone call. There is no point in advertising if one does not have both the material and the staff time for adequate follow-up.

Where do you advertise? To some extent this depends upon on how much you target. If, unlike the majority of agencies, you have targeted with great specificity, you might consider a trade journal. For example, if you are convinced that your city or county is just the right place for an injection molding operation, consider a trade journal in the plastics field. Your per reader costs will be much higher than if you advertise in a more general publication, but you will be reaching the people you want to reach.

If you do not target with much precision, the basic choice is between a magazine such as *Area Development*, which is targeted to a readership that makes location decisions, and a consumer publication. In the latter category are newspapers and magazines such as *Time* and *Newsweek*. Many magazines, such as *Time*, sell advertising space on a regional as well as a national basis. Thus a finer degree of geographic targeting is possible. On a per reader basis, a consumer publication is less expensive. For example, at this writing a full-page, black-and-white ad in *Time* would be about $77,000 and the circulation is about 4.3 million. This yields a cost of somewhat less than two cents per copy. *Area Development*, probably the best-known of the economic development publications, has a circulation of about 32,000 and charges close to $4,000 for a full-page, one-time, black-and-white ad. Thus the per copy cost is over ten cents. On the other hand, the quality of responses from a specialized publication will be much higher. Many specialized publications are "controlled circulation." Though the publication has a listed selling price, most copies are not sold. Rather, they are given to people whose job title qualifies them to receive the publication and who request it. The magazine makes almost all of its money from advertising. It appeals to advertisers because it offers a highly selected readership.

The writer's experience was that advertising in a specialized publication yielded more useful inquiries, though fewer total inquiries, per dollar spent. In addition, with a specialized publication one will spend less time and money on inquiries that do not promise any payoff—for example, high school students writing term papers.

Though full-page rates were cited above, third-page or quarter-page ads may be more cost effective. All that the ad needs to do is elicit sufficient interest to cause the reader to check off the number on the reader inquiry card. Unlike consumer advertising, the ad does not sell the "product." It simply makes a connection that the agency follows up.

One way to proceed with advertising would be to try fractional page ads in several publications, observe the quality and quantity of inquiries, and then make some decision about which publication(s) seem most cost effective. But note that the law of diminishing returns will apply to the same or similar ad run repeatedly in the same publication. Thus there is some logic to spreading one's advertising around rather than concentrating it, regardless of what the advertising salesman for a particular publication may tell you about the need for repetition.

OUTREACH

As suggested in Chapter 6, one of the more important and productive activities for most development agencies is outreach to the existing business establishment. Not only can outreach foster expansion of firms now in the community, but it offers defense against the predatory activities of one's colleagues.

One generally cannot reach out to the entire business community, so some selection is necessary. One category that should be assigned high priority is whichever section of the local economy appears to have most growth potential. Another is whichever sector appears to be most footloose. As noted before, this is likely to be some area of manufacturing, for many manufacturers sell to a national market and therefore have a wide choice of potential locations. If the economic development program has been done after a careful analysis of labor market conditions and with specific labor market goals in mind, then outreach may be directed to firms that employ particular categories of workers. As noted earlier, this sort of careful analysis, though praiseworthy, is not done very often.

One way to approach firms is with a letter followed by a phone call to see whether a meeting is worthwhile. A colleague of the author did very well with a letter that began "How can we help you? We are the . . . ."

It cannot be overemphasized that the workings of government often appear quite opaque to firms. This is particularly so of smaller firms where all personnel have operating responsibilities and there are no purely staff people who have time to research questions. At one time, the writer had dealings with a small jobber in aircraft parts. The firm distributed various fittings, fasteners, seals. It generally received a truckload of parts per day and shipped them out in small packages by parcel post. In terms of impact on the community, it was little different from a small office. The firm owned land and wanted to expand on it. Unfortunately, the zoning law specified that no more than 25 percent of floor space might be warehousing. The firm, needing to store a large inventory, required a facility that was 75 percent storage and 25 percent offices—the reverse of what the zoning permitted. The firm's needs, though they clearly violated the letter of the law, did not violate the intent of the law. But, because of the problem, the firm was on the verge of moving. The author's agency counseled the firm on how to present its case to the zoning board and then wrote a rough draft of an appeal from the firm to the board. Without too much delay, a zoning variance was obtained. On another occasion, the owner of a small manufacturing firm indicated to the writer that he intended to move his operation out of New York State and into the adjacent state of Connecticut. On inquiry, it turned out that the firm was expanding and had to move from its present quarters. The reason for moving to Connecticut was that Connecticut offered tax-exempt financing through the Connecticut Development

Authority. After the owner described the financing package offered, the writer asked whether he was aware that essentially the same package was available in New York State. The answer was "no," and the move was forestalled. Had the contact not occurred until after the owner signed a contract on property in Connecticut, the firm would have moved. Early contacts with companies are thus essential.

DIRECT SELLING

For many agencies there is no separate, direct selling operation. The agency simply responds to inquiries. These may be inquiries that would have come to the agency even if it made no effort to make itself visible, or they may result from its public relations and advertising efforts or from personal contacts within the community, or they may be referrals from state agencies.

For the agency that does some direct, outside selling, one technique is to pick target industries by analysis of the community's strengths and weaknesses, and then locate appropriate firms. Usually the easiest way to find firms is through an industrial directory that lists the firm, its assets, its main lines of business, and its top personnel. Dun and Bradstreet is a common source. After a target list has been drawn up, contact is made with the firm. One common approach is a letter followed by a phone call.

A variation on this theme employed by one economic development consultant is to use firms in the area as a source of leads to their customers and suppliers. A principal in the local firm may be persuaded to write or call or to let the consultant draft a letter for his or her signature. According to the consultant, a letter coming from someone who is known to the recipient generally is more effective than a letter from a stranger.

Some economic development agencies will make "cold calls." A representative of the agency simply knocks on the doors of firms without an appointment. However, the logistics of this are prohibitive unless there are large numbers of firms in close physical proximity. A densely developed urban area is thus most suitable to this sort of prospecting.

Trade shows are another venue for prospecting. This presumes that the agency has targeted the industry or industries represented at the show. One caution is that travel, lodging, renting floor space, and setting up a booth can be expensive. If a particular industry has been targeted, the cost of attending a trade show might be weighed against the alternative of advertising in the appropriate trade magazine. One problem with the trade show approach is that many of the people one will meet are not in the position to make location decisions. For example, if one attends the Institute of Electrical and Electronic Engineers show, one will meet large numbers of engineers. Whether one will meet large numbers of directors of corporate planning or large numbers of chief executive officers—the people who are likely to make the location decision—is more problematic. The focus of the show is technical, and the mind-set of the attendees may not be particularly attuned to questions of business location. Without attempting to be definitive, let us simply note that if targeting studies have been done, trade show attendance is certainly worth exploring.

Trade fairs that a large number of firms from many different industries attend are also a possibility. For these, one does not need to have done targeting studies. One checks the roster of attendees and proceeds from there. These fairs can be used either domestically or for overseas prospecting. As noted previously, few of the economic developers surveyed by the author showed much enthusiasm for overseas prospecting. One item to be considered with overseas prospecting is the cost.

THE DATABASE

The purpose of advertising, like that of public relations, is to begin a dialogue between firm and development agency. The agency must have a solid factual basis from which to conduct its side of the dialogue. It should have a substantial amount of material it can give to the firm "off the shelf," and it should have the personnel and familiarity with the community so that it can find the answers to questions quickly. Until the database and the facility to answer questions are in place, advertising should not be done. A campaign that is not backed by real substance will irritate people and make the agency look frivolous.

Below is a general list of items that should be considered for the community database. Not all need be provided for every community. Conversely, the community may have special assets that will not appear on this list but that should be made visible. After the list, we turn to the matter of presentation.

1. *Demographic information.* This includes basic information on total population, age structure of the population, educational levels, recent growth trends, and personal income. If the place is large or composed of a number of municipalities, it may be useful to provide some information on how this population is physically distributed. It is not necessary to provide exhaustive detail such as is to be found in the census.

2. *Labor market information.* This is a profile of the labor force cast in terms of numbers, occupations, skills, and educational levels. Unemployment rates and labor force participation rates should be included. If the data are available, wage levels for particular job classifications should be presented.

3. *Data on the existing business community.* This should include employment by industry. If there are prominent firms in the community, a list of major corporations present can be a big selling point. If IBM or Xerox is prospering in your community, that suggests that other firms can, too. It also suggests that the de-

cision makers in prestigious companies looked at your community and thought well of it. This can be very reassuring to the decision maker. For business services such a listing is a roster of potential clients.

4. *Transportation facilities.* Highways, railroads, airports, and port facilities should be presented in adequate detail. Some information on time and distance to major market areas also may be useful.

5. *Utilities.* Utilities and their service areas should be shown. Utility rate structures can be complex, but some approximations should be given—for example, an approximate cents-per-kilowatt-hour figure for industrial or commercial users.

6. *Business cost data.* Land costs, commercial rents, construction costs, and cost of living should be provided if reasonably accurate data are available.

7. *Taxes.* Both personal and business taxes should be listed. If the area compares favorably with competing areas, comparative data should be included.

8. *Financing assistance.* Local programs as well as state and federal programs to which the development agency can guide the firm should be listed and briefly described.

9. *Quality-of-life issues.* This is an increasingly important factor. Information should be provided on all levels of education, recreation, cultural facilities, housing cost and availability, climate, and public safety. If the community or its environs offers what appears to be an attractive living environment, this is a major selling point.

10. *Sites.* Some information on commercial and industrial sites is usually part of the database. In a small community with a very limited supply of sites, it may be possible to list all of them. In a large place some compromise may be advisable. For example, major industrial and commercial parks and areas in which there are substantial amounts of commercial floor space or large blocks of undeveloped land might be listed. The extent of the listing of sites also depends upon the agency's relationship with the commercial real estate community. Obviously, one wants to avoid conflict with commercial and industrial brokers. Then, too, if the commercial brokerage industry is active and competent, the agency's role in showing and listing specific sites need not be large.

11. *Regulatory and business climate.* Within the bounds of truthfulness it is important to present a friendly and welcoming picture. Information on labor legislation such as right-to-work laws (something of an ideological litmus test for many employers), land-use controls, and environmental regulations should be presented.

12. *Specialized facilities for industry.* If the community or its environs offers any facilities not found everywhere, for example, a hazardous-waste disposal facility, these should be noted.

How the above and similar data are presented will depend upon the amount of data and the funds available for packaging. Many communities, as well as states, produce a general brochure that presents a relatively brief picture in an attractive, readable manner. A moment spent marking the reader inquiry card at the back of a publication like *Area Development* or *Plants, Sites and Parks* will bring the reader a large supply of samples. The brochure is meant to be suitable for mailing or handing out at meetings or events. It typically presents a moderate amount of the above information and often some material to create an image. The image material may be pictures of scenery or recreation, testimonials from businessmen now in the area about what a good business location it is, and so on.

A number of agencies produce audiovisual equivalents of the brochure that are suitable for showing in the office or at gatherings. The writer has not had direct experience with these and thus is not in a position to testify about their effectiveness. The obvious question is whether, if the prospect is in the office, the audiovisual is really needed. In any case, audiovisuals cannot take the place of printed material.

The agency should maintain detailed material to be used in response to specific inquiry. Much of this can be done with maps and data sheets. Population distribution can be shown with dot maps. Unless the entire area has water and sewer, those areas served can be mapped, and main sewer and water lines shown. A map showing highways and rail and other transportation facilities is essential. Many retailers and service businesses are interested in traffic flow, so a map showing traffic volumes (generally expressed as average annual daily traffic) can be useful. Maps that show zoning and the community's master plan should be provided. If the agency plans to present information on particular sites, these should be located on a map of the community. Whether individual maps should also be provided to show site geometry, topography, details of road access, and so on depends upon how deeply the agency intends to go into the marketing of sites. If the agency decides to go very deeply, all of the above plus ownership, area, assessed value, zoning classification, distance to utilities, subsoil conditions, and drainage should be provided for each site.

Many agencies produce a folder with inside pockets into which maps, data sheets, and flyers can be inserted. The package of information can then be tailored to the recipient. A standard logo on the folder and other materials gives the complete package a distinct identity.

For sites, the computerized database is coming into use. A large amount of data is stored and then can be explored in response to particular needs. If the prospect says that he or she needs a site of fifty acres or more with manufacturing zoning and a rail siding, those requirements are entered and a listing of suitable sites comes back. Whether such a database is worth building depends upon how often it is to be used. The front-end costs are significant.

The writer was involved in building a database in the mid-1980s for a large, thriving suburban county located in the southeast. A base of about 1,500 sites cost $56,000 to build. Most of the cost was for student labor to check maps, visit sites, examine assessors' records, and so on. Altogether, about three person-years of student labor and several months of supervisory labor went into the project. The price was something of a bargain because the student labor was relatively low wage and the university, which served as consultant and general contractor on the project, charged a much lower overhead factor than would a private consultant. A current estimate for a comparable base developed by a consultant might approach $100,000.

When the director of the agency was questioned about it in the summer of 1989, he indicated that it had been money well spent. The database is used to locate potential sites both for prospects in the office and for distant inquiries. In addition, it is used to assist local real estate brokers who call with a request for a site that meets certain characteristics (size, zoning, access, and such). The agency enters the specified characteristics and sends the resulting printout to the broker. It is hard to imagine a better device for building a harmonious relationship with the real estate brokerage industry. The agency reports an average of about two inquiries a day.

The main expenditure of time for the database is updating. As sewers are extended, properties reassessed, parcels sold or developed, these items must be entered into the system to keep it current. Clearly, an important system design consideration is that it can be updated by personnel who do not necessarily have much computer experience. According to the agency's director, the only thing he would do differently were he doing it again is that the number of data items per site would be smaller. As it stands, the database contains about eighty items per site, apparently more than is required to zero in on sites that are worth further examination.

Given the increases in the power of the personal computer and the large amount of good, low-priced software on the market, a simple database does not require large expenditures on machinery or programming. If graphics capability is not required, a PC and some off-the-shelf software will be quite adequate. A database program like DBase or even a spreadsheet such as SuperCalc or Lotus may be quite sufficient. For example, if the goal is to store, let us say, forty data items (map coordinates, zoning, area, assessed value, distance to nearest highway, distance to nearest trunk sewer, and such) on a few hundred sites, almost any spreadsheet or database program will be adequate. Most are relatively user friendly and should not take more than a few days for most agency personnel to master.

If a spreadsheet program is used, new sites are entered simply by typing in a new line on the spreadsheet. Data on old sites are updated by editing one or more cells on the line for that site. If a database program is used, new sites are entered by creating a new record and old sites are updated by editing existing records. Thus the mechanics of updating are simple and do not require much in the way of computer skills.

Graphic capabilities are impressive, but they may not be necessary. Once the system has located the sites that meet the specifications of the inquiry, it is no great trouble to walk to the file cabinet and pull out the appropriate maps.

9

Assessing Economic Development Potential

The most appropriate place to begin planning an economic development program is a realistic assessment of the development potential of the area. Such an assessment provides guidance for the expenditure of the development agency's necessarily limited money, energy, and legal and political powers. No initial assessment will prove entirely accurate. As the economic developer has contact with firms, brokers, bankers, property owners, and others, his or her insight into the area will increase. Unanticipated strengths and opportunities, weaknesses and problems, will emerge. Thus, like most plans, the initial assessment is meant to be modified. Nonetheless, a general assessment of the area's strengths and weaknesses should be undertaken either before the agency is founded or, if not, early in the history of the agency. Once the agency is in full operation, time for research and planning will be hard to come by.

A systematic evaluation of the area's strengths and weaknesses will not only help in planning, but will also provide a basis for justifying, defending, and explaining the program, both to the public and within the councils of government. An unrealistic view of an area's potential leads to wasted effort, expectations that cannot be met, and ultimate disillusionment. Admittedly, the political climate is often such that the economic developer cannot be absolutely candid with his or her employers or the citizenry in general. A certain note of obligatory optimism seems to come with the territory. But he or she can at least look at the facts as objectively as possible for internal purposes.

As noted earlier, most economic development agencies are likely to accomplish more through the nurturing of existing industry than through the recruitment of new industry. Thus it is important to consider strengths and weaknesses from the perspective of the existing business establishment as well as of new firms.

How detailed an assessment is necessary depends upon the potential scope of the program. If the program is a small one, let us say a three- or four-person operation, that will focus almost entirely upon dissemination of information and outreach to existing firms, a "quick and dirty" but realistic assessment may be sufficient. More detailed and searching analysis may not be cost effective. If significant money and effort are to be devoted to outside recruiting, then a more detailed assessment should be made so that these outside efforts can be effectively targeted.

One way to proceed is to characterize strengths and weaknesses of the community. Then these strengths and weaknesses can be compared with what is known about the requirements of various types of industry.

STRENGTHS AND WEAKNESSES

Location and Transportation

This is a question that has a number of dimensions.[1] On a large scale, one should consider access to major metropolitan areas. One commonly used statistic is population within "overnight trucking distance." The term does not have a precise meaning, but for an area with reasonable access to an interstate highway, one might calculate the population within a 500-mile radius. For other than heavy industry, at the time of this writing, highway accessibility is more important than access by any other means.

Since the first edition of this book appeared, the real cost of motor fuel has declined and the dispersal of economic activity and population has continued. Whether either shortages of fuel or policy changes promoted by concern with the greenhouse effect and consequent climatic change will push up the real costs of motor fuel remains to be seen. If this does happen, it may well favor locations that have rail access. On a ton/mile basis rail is three to four times as fuel efficient as truck transportation.

For truck access vis-à-vis other areas, the key issue is proximity to the interstate highway system. So many communities have good access that such access is hardly a decisive advantage. Lack of access, however, may be a very formidable disadvantage.

Some evaluation of rail access should be made. Links and distances to major concentrations of population can readily be determined from maps. Beyond that, some determination should be made as to whether there are any special limitations. For example, trailer on flatcar is a particularly economical way to ship for many firms because it retains much of the flexibility of trucking while achieving the lower per-mile costs of rail. But it requires larger clearances on tunnels and overpasses, and special loading and unloading facilities. A few conversations with shippers will turn up particular and nonobvious, but often significant, details.

As a determinant of economic location, water transportation is generally less significant than either truck or rail, except in a limited number of industries where bulk transportation costs are very significant. (Barge and freighter are the most energy-efficient modes on a ton-mile basis.) Nonetheless, for a place with a coastal or river location, the question should not be ignored. Beyond what can be seen from looking at maps, some inquiry should be made as to limitations posed by channel depths and loading facilities. For example, not every port that can accommodate oceangoing vessels has the facilities to accept containerized freight. San Francisco is a case in point.

On a ton/mile basis, pipeline costs are comparable with water transport costs. Obviously, the range of commodities that can be moved by pipeline is limited.

Access by air also should be considered. Here, one should break the inquiry into two parts. One is the condition of scheduled service to major destinations. The other is the presence and adequacy of general aviation facilities. For a number of types of activity, adequate access by air is essential. The point is discussed in more detail later in this chapter.

After considering access with regard to other areas, access within the area in question should be considered. Does the area in question have an advantage or disadvantage vis-à-vis competing places in the same area? For example, in the New York area, two suburban counties, Nassau and Suffolk, with a combined population of about 2.5 million, are located on Long Island. Their only road access to the rest of the United States is through New York City via bridges and tunnels. In spite of good labor forces, somewhat lower-than-average wage rates for the region, available land, and many quality-of-life advantages, the two counties have generally been unable to compete with other suburban counties in the region for many types of office and manufacturing employment. The access problem is apparently the main, if not the only, reason. This type of intra-area access advantage or disadvantage will generally be apparent from maps or from the experience of living in the area. But, again, a few conversations with major employers and shippers may ferret out aspects of the situation that are not immediately apparent.

Labor Markets

Most studies of industrial location indicate that the two biggest considerations in making a general choice of area are access to markets and access to labor.[2] (Within a given area, other factors will then determine the final choice of municipality and site.) This statement has been becoming truer with the passage of time and will probably continue to do so. This is because the cost of transport of both raw materials and finished or semi-finished goods has been declining in importance. Primary industries like steel, lumber, and cement, for which material costs are typically an important item, have been declining as a percentage of total economic activity and employment. Then, too, the per-pound value of many manufactured goods has been rising as goods have gotten both lighter and more sophisticated.

At least four dimensions of the labor market should be considered: wage rates, quality, availability, and unionization and legislation.

The most useful wage comparisons are those which show typical wages for different areas by occupation. Nationally, the best source for such information is provided by the *Area Wage Surveys*.[3] These provide average wages, median wages, and hours worked for about forty different occupations, for major metropolitan areas. They are useful in determining a particular area's wage-rate competitiveness when starting a development program, and may also be useful later in preparing promotional materials and/or a database (see Chapter 8). Within any given state, some of the same types of material may be provided by state labor departments. Monthly wage comparisons on a state and a major-labor-market basis are available in *Employment and Earnings*.[4] Unfortunately, they are limited to an average figure for production workers in manufacturing establishments.

Like most other sources of data on wages, the *Area Wage Surveys* focus on jobs that are relatively standardized and therefore comparable. Forklift operators in Chicago do very much the same work as forklift operators in Fargo, North Dakota. The same is not necessarily true for attorneys or managers. Thus, when one considers managerial, professional, and some technical workers, firm statistical comparability is not possible, and one is thrown back on the impressions of employers, personnel directors, and employment agency personnel. But impressions often determine decisions, so a little time spent gathering such impressions should prove worthwhile.

For an overview of trends in labor markets nationally, there are a number of publications available. Two that may be useful are *Manpower Review* and *Occupational Outlook*, both published by the Bureau of Labor Statistics, Department of Labor.

Labor-force quality is the most subjective of the four labor dimensions listed earlier. In some development advertising, one will see value added per worker put forth as an indicator of labor-force quality. In reality, this is a measure of capital intensity more than anything else. Number of years of education of the adult population (a census data item) is sometimes used as a measure of overall labor-force quality. Its meaning is questionable. Not only is the statistic not available by occupation, but beyond that, the link between years of schooling and job performance is not necessarily a rigid one. Here, perhaps more than in any other area, we are thrown back on impressions. Employers' perceptions of labor quality are a major factor in decision making and thus are worth gathering.

Even within relatively small areas, employers may perceive large differences in labor-force quality. The writer, working in a county of 450 square miles, was surprised to find that manufacturers saw large qualitative differences in the labor markets of communities only a few miles apart. These were differences that were in no way apparent from any available statistics, and yet the views of different employers were sufficiently consistent to convince the writer that they represented something real.

Some data on the labor force and its composition in terms of major categories of workers are available from the decennial census. The census is taken in years ending with 0 and published statistics become available in the following year. Fortunately, for most areas the occupational mix of the population will not change abruptly over the period, so that this type of data does not age too rapidly. Then, too, as one gets further away in time from the last census, some projections can be made.

Unemployment rates are another dimension of labor availability. At the county and municipal level they are generally available from state labor departments. The overall rate conveys some meaning, and rates by occupation, if available, convey more. But one should not make too much of the number of workers apparently available on the basis of unemployment figures. For many firms, the size of the labor pool is a better indication of long-term availability than is the apparent number of available workers on a given day. For one thing, hiring is a competitive process. For a second, the size of the labor force is somewhat flexible. Within the geographical area, workers move into and out of the labor pool and move from one category of work to another within the pool. Then, too, job availability promotes migration.

When the writer was engaged in economic development in a suburb whose population was growing slowly, but that was experiencing very rapid growth of corporate headquarters activity, all available data showed very tight markets for secretarial and clerical workers. In a period in which the female working-age population grew by perhaps 40 percent, clerical and secretarial employment in the area nearly doubled. From looking at numbers, it seemed inevitable that shortages of such workers were on the verge of choking off further corporate growth. Yet new corporate headquarters continued to move in and generally reported satisfaction with the labor market. The labor supply was obviously much more elastic than the statistics suggested. What was happening? New firms, by offering additional jobs, pushed up female labor-force participation rates. In addition, county residents who had previously worked outside the county began working closer to home. Finally, in-commutation from adjacent counties that had experienced relatively faster population growth, but relatively slower corporate headquarters growth, increased. A damaging shortfall in secretarial and clerical labor was always imminent but never materialized. Labor-force calculations are of considerable interest and use, but it must be remembered that the size of the labor force is not an absolutely rigid quantity. (The other side of this point, as noted earlier, is that employment gains may lower unemployment rates less than expected.)

Another source of insight into labor-market conditions is provided by job banks maintained by state employment agencies. Such banks may contain information on job vacancies posted by employers and on the occupations of job seekers. Also available from state labor departments are data on the characteristics of unemployment insurance recipients.[5] These data can be used to quickly locate occupations in which there are obvious labor surpluses.

Finally, at the risk of repetition, the economic developer trying to assemble a picture of his or her area's labor market would do well to talk with employers and employment agencies. Those who are involved daily in the labor market often have insights that are not obtainable from statistics alone. Given the generally favorable growth attitudes of businessmen, the economic developer should have little difficulty persuading local employers to communicate with him or her.

Both unionization and protective labor legislation perform many useful functions. Making an area attractive to potential employers is not, however, one of these functions. In general, whether a city or state is a strong union area will be well known to both management and labor. The economic developer will have little difficulty ascertaining his or her area's reputation. New York, Pennsylvania, and New England, for example, are generally regarded as strong union areas. Most southern states are not. If hard data on the degree of unionization are required, they can be obtained from the *Statistical Abstract of the United States*.

The situation regarding labor legislation, from the economic developer's point of view, can readily be determined by communication with employers, unions, and state labor departments. One piece of legislation that has become quite well known is the right-to-work law. Essentially, this forbids making union membership a condition of employment; that is, it prohibits the union shop. It is typically found in states of a generally conservative political complexion, for example, Kansas. It would be anathema in a state of strongly liberal persuasion, such as Massachusetts. Many of those states which have such legislation trumpet this fact in their advertising regarding economic development. In the writer's view, it is probably more important to potential employers, as a kind of ideological litmus test than as a thing in itself.

Other labor-related legislation of a less general and less well-known nature may be of some import to the economic developer. For example, only New York and Rhode Island pay unemployment insurance benefits to strikers. As one corporation representative told the writer, in explaining why the firm was thinking of pulling a particular operation out of New York State: "We have branches in many states. When we have a strike, our New York branch is always the last to settle." The law happens to be a red flag to many businessmen, partly because of the reason suggested and partly because of the idea that employers' contributions to the unemployment insurance fund are being used to subsidize strikes. In the case of the firm mentioned above, the writer's organization obtained advantageous tax-exempt financing for it, and the firm, rather than leaving, expanded. Whether the above comments on the law by the firm's spokesman were totally ingenuous, or sprang from a desire to motivate the writer, is known only by the speaker. As in the case of the right-to-work law, one suspects that specific legislation favoring labor or management means more to employers as a sign of political climate than it does strictly for its own sake.

Quality of Life

Though obviously a subjective area, there is no doubt that employers' perceptions of quality of life are important in locational decisions involving activities in which access to raw materials or bulk transportation costs are not major factors. It is particularly true of activities in which ability to recruit specialized personnel is important. In short, it is a major factor in the location of corporate headquarters, many types of service businesses, firms engaged in research and development or other high-technology activities, and in some types of manufacturing other than heavy industry. As noted earlier, improvements in transportation and communication, combined with increased personal income, have made quality-of-life issues more important relative to the more traditional determinants of economic location. Climate and physical environment are obviously important factors. California's warm air and beaches and Colorado's ski slopes are significant factors in attracting many types of activity.

Housing markets within the commuting range of a proposed site may be an important consideration. This is true primarily for the firm that expects either to bring with it many of its present personnel or to have to recruit many personnel who are not now area residents. When office operations are moved, it is common to expect very high attrition rates among secretarial, clerical, and custodial personnel—people who are believed to have commonly found skills and who can be replaced without great disruption to operations. But most companies will make strenuous efforts to keep managerial and technical personnel, part of whose value to the company is their familiarity with its operations. It is at this point that the firm will begin looking at housing markets and asking how much it will cost to relocate personnel to a particular housing market. High prices and long commutes will mean higher wages, bigger relocation costs, and more refusals to be transferred. Similarly, a manufacturer who requires skilled technical work that cannot be done by the resident labor force will begin to wonder whether he can get new workers to move into the area. One force behind the relocation of corporate headquarters from central city to suburb has been the attraction of the suburban housing stock. Objective housing data are available from the decennial census. More current but less objective impressions can be had from realtors, tax commissions, assessors, the real estate ads, and direct observation.

The quality of education is a major consideration in relocation for several reasons. One is its implication for labor-force quality. One industrial location consultant, in a report on the potential market for office space in a major city, wrote the following: "From the businessman's viewpoint, there is considerable doubt that the . . . public high schools are producing the quality of graduates needed to operate modern, sophisticated offices. One-half of all graduates receive general diplomas on completion of their twelfth year, failing to meet qualifications for an academic diploma. As some educators have summarized the problem, students are passed from one grade to the next merely because they have become one year older."

Some of the exodus of firms from central-city locations is explainable in terms of such perceptions as that above. The question is also wrapped up in the matter of central-city racial and ethnic change.

A second dimension of the question is education for the children of company personnel. A good public school system is a key recruiting asset. Poor public schools to which middle- and upper-management personnel are reluctant to send their children can be a major discouragement to recruitment. In some cases, managerial personnel may refuse transfer to such locations. In other cases, the cost of private school tuition may be capitalized in the higher salaries necessary to get personnel to accept transfer. In general, the quality of public education will be well known. If quantitative information is needed, achievement test scores and other comparative data on school districts can be obtained from state education departments.

The presence of opportunities for higher education is also a powerful consideration in the location of certain types of activity—particularly high-technology firms. The presence of MIT in the Boston area has been a major factor in the ability of that city to attract electronics firms. It is doubtful whether the concentration of high-technology firms on Route 128 (a circumferential highway around Boston) would exist were it not for the presence of MIT. A considerable number of firms indicated that a factor causing them to locate in the New York suburbs was the existence in the city of Columbia, New York University, the City University, and other schools at which their people could pursue graduate education.

Public Safety

Fear of crime is a major deterrent to commercial and industrial location. The same consultant's report quoted earlier noted, "Probably no single factor has greater impact on the ability to hold middle-management families ... than fears relating to security of person and property." Fear of crime takes different forms for different types of activities. For a retailer, it may be primarily that customers will be kept away. For an insurance company, it may be that it will be impossible to recruit women to work on evening shifts. Manufacturing firms located in deteriorating urban areas may find that fear of arson and difficulties in obtaining fire insurance cause them to think seriously about relocating.

In many cases the situation, whether favorable or unfavorable, will be so generally well understood that the economic developer will have no need to do any special research on this subject. If he or she feels that hard data are needed, some statistics are available from the federal government.[6]

Cost of Living

Cost of living tends to be capitalized in wage rates, but wages, of course, can be tracked down directly. Thus cost of living is not directly relevant when thinking about workers one does not expect to relocate with the firm. On the other hand, it can be highly relevant in considering managerial or technical workers the firm must keep in order to function. To induce a middle-management worker earning, say, $50,000 per year to move from Des Moines to Fairfax County, Virginia, or Fairfield County, Connecticut, without a very substantial raise is asking the worker to accept a deep cut in living standard. In the late 1970s and 1980s, when house prices rose more rapidly than personal income, the housing cost issue became particularly important.

Until the early 1980s the Bureau of Labor Statistics published typical family budgets for major metropolitan areas. Unfortunately, this series has been discontinued, and it is now very difficult to obtain good comparative data. The one exception to this is housing, for statistics on rents and house values can still be obtained from both the decennial census and the annual census of housing. However, a word of caution is necessary here. The household moving into the area may find that in actual practice it confronts higher prices and rents than the data indicate, for what is on the market at a given time may be well above the average for the entire housing stock.

Commutation and Transportation

This question is of importance mainly in large metropolitan areas. The prospect of a long commute is a discouragement to executive and professional recruitment and also may shorten workweeks. The 9-to-5 office workday in some major cities, in contrast with the 8-to-5 workday in many smaller places, is in part a concession to the longer commute. Long commuting times between suburbs and downtown business districts are another reason for the suburbanization of much office activity.

Political Climate

Political climate is another subjective yet important consideration. As the size of the government sector grows, and particularly as the regulatory power of government grows, the political climate as perceived by the would-be industrial or commercial resident becomes increasingly important. The force and flexibility with which land-use controls and environmental controls are applied are often critical. Many firms display a near paranoia on the subject of environmentally based litigation, and there is some substance behind the fears. The firm tied up in litigation regarding, say, a discharge permit or a zoning change watches interest charges and capital costs mount while competitors walk off with former or potential customers. The fact that environmental and public-interest groups often seize the moral high ground adds a dimension of public relations disaster to many such confrontations. A few articulate and well-organized citizens, with a talent for public relations and enough money to afford first-rate legal counsel, can inspire fear in the heart of any corporation president.

Political conservatism is reassuring to many firms because it suggests a generally favorable business attitude and a relative absence of litigation, delay, and confrontation. It cannot be quantified, but it is reasonable to assume and widely believed that the generally more conservative political temper of the South has been an advantage in bidding business away from the more liberal Northeast.

Cost and Availability of Utilities

Electric rates should be compared with the national average and with those in competing locations. The structure of electric rates is complicated for commercial customers, varying with amount consumed, time of consumption, and maximum rate of consumption. At this stage, a comparison based on average cost per kilowatt-hour to commercial and industrial customers should be sufficient.[7]

Natural gas availability should be determined. In the 1970s and early 1980s natural gas had a considerable cost advantage, often as much as two to one, over petroleum. With the almost complete deregulation of natural gas, market forces have tended to bring petroleum and gas prices closer and to erase much of this advantage. While the cost advantage of gas is diminished, it still does have environmental advantages in that it burns cleaner than fuel oil.

On a BTU/dollar basis, coal has a considerable cost advantage over both natural gas and petroleum. However, it is much more of an environmental villain both because of the emission of pollutants such as sulfur dioxide and because burning coal produces more carbon dioxide per BTU than does burning either petroleum or natural gas. While the other pollutants may be dealt with, albeit expensively, the higher carbon dioxide emission is inherent in the chemistry of the fuel and cannot be changed. How heavily coal burning will be regulated, particularly in the light of growing concern with the greenhouse effect, remains to be seen.

Tax Burden

No complete statement on tax burden is possible because the same tax structure will look different to every firm. No tax has yet been devised that falls equally on all taxpayers. However, some general data should be developed for the area. The two statistics most commonly used for states are total tax burden per capita and taxes as a percentage of total income. A profile of tax burden within the area should also be developed. This includes personal taxes (on income and on personal property), sales taxes, and business taxes (on corporate income, capital gains, personal property, inventory). The range of business taxes in the United States is quite large. Taxes in particular areas may include commercial occupancy, gross receipts, unincorporated business taxes, and others.

For interstate comparisons, the *Statistical Abstract of the United States* and the *Census of Governments*, both published by the Bureau of the Census, will provide adequate information. Property taxes per capita and total tax burdens for cities and counties can be found in the *County and City Data Book*, another Census Bureau publication. For intrastate purposes, however, the most convenient and comprehensive source in most cases will be the state yearbook or data book. Annual reports by state controllers' offices are also useful.

Land Availability, Land-Use Controls, and Development Costs

For vacant land under existing zoning categories, the best source is often the area's planning agency. Failing that, municipal engineers and assessors are good sources. Zoning, however, should be viewed with a certain sophistication by the economic developer. The reality may or may not be what the map and ordinance indicate. For example, in many suburban areas, a talk with those who have been around the planning scene for some time will reveal that numerous shopping centers, industrial parks, and corporate headquarters now stand on land that was zoned as single-family residential at the time they were proposed. Communities use the device of such zoning to keep land out of development until a fiscally and otherwise attractive proposal is made. At this point, rezoning occurs. Such a strategy also allows the community to bargain with developers over site design and other matters, whereas if land were zoned as commercial in the first instance, construction would take place as a matter of right, without such bargaining. On the other side of the coin, the writer is aware of at least one community in which hundreds of acres without water and sewer connections, and with a generally forbidding topography, are zoned as industrial. The zoning in this case has the effect (probably unintentional) of providing open space at no municipal cost. Landowners resist residential offers for fear of losing the opportunity of selling to industry at a higher price, but few firms show any interest in locating there.

Finally, in considering land availability, the economic developer should be aware of physical constraints. As a general rule of thumb, commercial construction on slopes over 5 percent (5-foot rise per 100 feet horizontally) is uneconomic. However, in areas where the cost of the best land is very high, construction will occur on steeper slopes, with steepness traded for lower land costs. Remoteness from water and sewer lines is an obstacle to development. Landlocked parcels (without direct road access) may appear in planning agency land inventories, yet the chance of their being developed may be remote. In recent years, wetland and floodplain zoning has rendered many areas undevelopable.

Thus, any off-the-shelf figure on available land should be tempered with some insight into both land-use control practice and physical reality.

Construction costs relative to other areas can be found in a number of construction handbooks often referred to as "cost calculators."[8] Such books, in addition to having a wealth of material of a technical nature, also have a city-cost index that gives relative costs for major cities. This can be used to make place-to-place comparisons. It can also be used to make rough project estimates. One takes the national cost per square foot given for the type of construction and modifies it by the appropriate city index.

Demographic Characteristics

Demographic characteristics are important to potential firms for various reasons and therefore deserve an initial look by the economic developer. A relatively brief consideration of census data will provide basic statistics, such as population size, labor-force characteristics (percentages of the labor force in various general occupational categories), personal income, and educational level of the adult population. To give them some meaning, they should be laid off against the same figures for the state and the nation and for competing communities.

MATCHING AREA CHARACTERISTICS TO FIRM NEEDS

Having reviewed the area characteristics, whether in a formal and structured way or otherwise, a logical next step is to begin thinking about how broad categories of economic activity and the area are suited to each other.

Categories to be discussed here are retailing, wholesaling and related operations, corporate headquarters, other large-office functions, research and development, business services, and manufacturing. Left out of this list are agriculture, extractive industries, and other activities tied to particular physical resources, terrain, or climatic features.

The predominant determinant of retailing location is demographic characteristics. Large retailers are among the most sophisticated business users of demographic data. Large retailing chains will often have on their staffs economists, statisticians, or others skilled in manipulating demographic data, estimating market shares, and projecting population growth. Smaller retailers are also very much motivated by demographic characteristics, though obviously their resources for manipulating data are not the same. Once the general choice of area is made, the next determinant is access or traffic flow. In big-city central business districts, pedestrian traffic flow may be the most important variable. In Manhattan, where the pattern is a grid of streets running east/west and of avenues running north/south, store rentals on avenues are substantially greater than on the streets because avenues have heavier pedestrian traffic. Proximity to a subway stop is capitalized in higher rents because of greater pedestrian traffic. In less densely developed areas, it is vehicular rather than pedestrian traffic that is paramount.

In terms of assessing whether substantial amounts of retailing can be attracted, the place to start is with demographic characteristics, particularly personal income. The second question is whether there exists unsatisfied demand. In the writer's opinion, the best way to determine this is informally. Just observe behavior and, perhaps, ask people where they shop for various types of goods. If there are categories of goods that cannot be bought locally, this will be readily apparent and will raise the question of whether this "leakage" from the local economy can be stopped.

It is possible to approach this question in a more formal manner by comparing income statistics from the decennial census with retail sales statistics from the Census of Retailing. One might then compare the ratio of sales to income in one's own area with that of the state or the nation to see whether there appears to be a net outflow. However, this approach is fraught with methodological problems and is probably less reliable than simple, direct observation.

If leakage of retail sales can be stopped, then the local economy will be stimulated. However, if there is no leakage and new retailing simply takes sales from established retailers, there has been no aggregate gain. In that case, pursuing retail growth does not achieve much. Here, the economic developer and the prospective retailer will have different perspectives. Unless there is some net outflow to be stopped, or there are outside sales to be captured, the economic developer may regard bringing in additional activity as playing a zero-sum game. The retailer, however, will naturally take a competitive rather than an aggregate view of the situation.

In the writer's view, public funds spent on assisting local retailing development are often almost totally wasted from the perspective of city- or countywide economic development. Of course, it is much easier to make this point in a book than it is at a public meeting. And it must be admitted that investing public funds in neighborhood retailing development may achieve other goals even if the aggregate effect on employment is zero.

Wholesaler location is partly dependent upon the presence of retailers. Therefore, in the growth process, the movement in of retailers often precedes the movement in of wholesalers. Good access for trucking is a major, if not the single most important, determinant of location for wholesalers. Neighborhood appearance and visibility are generally not important. Wholesaler location may be highly sensitive to land costs because warehouses, on a per-square-foot basis, are one of the least expensive forms of construction. Thus, land costs represent a higher percentage of the total cost. If zoning and other land-use controls mandate large setbacks or low coverage ratios for distributive activities, the sensitivity to land costs will be further increased.

Corporate headquarters are, in several ways, unique entities so far as locational choice is concerned. Questions of image and prestige play a larger role than in the location of any other type of activity. The corporate headquarters is a cost to be spread across the entirety of the corporation and is not viewed in a cold accounting light, as most other corporate functions are. The image question cannot be quantified, but it appears to weigh very heavily. The writer witnessed the subsidiary of a large European organization insist that its corporate headquarters be in a position to overlook Long Island Sound because its European headquarters overlooked a scenic body of water. Many economic developers can tell similar tales. The residential preferences of corporate executives also are likely to weigh heavily in the selection of the headquarters site. The people who make the decision about where to locate it are, generally, people who will be working in it.

Accessibility is a key determining item. In past years this decreed central-business-district locations. In the age of the automobile and the limited-access highway, most headquarters construction has been in the ring around the central city. The preferred combination for many is a bucolic-appearing site very close to the interchange of a major limited-access route. Air transportation is regarded as a necessity for many corporate headquarters. In some cases, access to an airport with good scheduled services is considered adequate. In other cases, proximity to a general aviation airport capable of handling corporate aircraft is required. There are several hundred airports in the United States that provide some scheduled air service, and probably no more than a few dozen airports that are considered hubs in the sense that they offer direct connections to a large number of other cities. On the other hand, there are well over 10,000 general aviation airports. Thus corporate aircraft can be a powerful economizer of executive time even if they fly much more slowly than commercial airliners. And, as it happens, the larger jet-powered corporate aircraft are not very far behind airliners in terms of speed and range. Corporate aviation also has something of a sales function. There is no better way to flatter a client or a prospect than by transporting him or her in a corporate aircraft. As a status symbol it is hard to surpass.

In the late 1970s the writer surveyed a number of corporations in the Westchester County-Fairfield County area regarding the importance of the Westchester County Airport, located at the border between these two large suburban counties. The field is a large general aviation airport with almost no scheduled service. There was no question that it was very important to many headquarters operations even though all three of the New York area airports—Newark, La Guardia, and JFK—were within an hour or so of the Westchester County Airport under normal traffic conditions.

The complex of issues discussed under the heading of quality of life appears to be important. This relates in part to the corporate-image question and in part to the matter of middle-management attraction and retention. Most corporate headquarters have substantial secretarial and clerical needs, so that labor-force availability is a significant factor. Closeness to business services appears to be important in inverse relationship to headquarters size. Not surprisingly, the large headquarters will internalize services that others contract out, and will thus be more independent in this regard. Land costs, construction costs, local taxes, and even wage rates do not appear to weigh as heavily as with many types of activity. This may be in part because the headquarters is overhead and is not treated as a profit center, as are other operations.

For other types of office activity, questions of prestige and image are likely to be less important. If the work is of a more routinized nature, such as processing insurance claims and policies, much less interaction with the outside world is required. Labor-force availability and quality, and wage rates are likely to be the most important locational factors. Utility and energy costs will probably be relatively minor considerations because they represent a very small fraction of total operating expense. A typical cost for utilities for a modern office building might be $2 per square foot per year. With, say, one worker per 300 gross square feet (a common figure), a variation of 25 percent from that ratio would result in a cost differential of $150 per worker per year, probably less than 0.50 percent of annual operating expense.

Research and development activities, in general, locate largely on the basis of labor-force availability and the opportunity for useful interaction with firms or organizations in related activities. Attractive climate, presence of recreational and cultural facilities, presence of major educational institutions, and presence of firms doing related work seem to be the dominant considerations. Being close to firms engaged in similar efforts entails the risks of losing key personnel through piracy and the leakage of proprietary information to competitors, but it also offers corresponding advantages along these same lines. More generally, there is likely to be a synergistic effect for everyone. The firm that is remote from a center of activity is likely to suffer from being out of touch. More traditional considerations, such as transportation costs, land costs, tax structure, and even wage rates, are likely to be much less important. The importance of the university connection cannot be overemphasized. The two centers of microelectronics activity in the United States were both heavily influenced by it. The Route 128 complex around Boston owes much of its existence to Harvard and MIT. The Silicon Valley complex owes much of its existence to Stanford. As noted in Chapter 4, comparable dynamics operated in the 1970s and early 1980s in the case of the genetic engineering industry.

It is important to be realistic in thinking about attracting R&D activity. Thousands of communities want it for evident reasons. It involves many well-paying jobs and it usually is environmentally benign. It holds out the prospect of bringing in superbright, energetic, entrepreneurial people who will start all sorts of spin-off businesses as soon as the technology they are working on achieves commercial potential.

"High-technology" is not as precise a term as "sheet metal fabrication" or "ferrous metals," but, however one defines it, the total number of people employed in high-technology activities is not vast. If one's area cannot offer the university connection, good quality of life, and good transportation (not for goods but for people going to conferences, to visit other firms, and so on), one is probably best advised to write it off. The competition from places that can offer these things is too formidable. This is not to say that high-technology firms do not spring up in unlikely places through the presence of highly talented individuals. However, it is to say that if the place does not have the characteristics noted above, the chances of recruiting high-technology activity from outside are extremely small.

Business services such as law, accounting, consulting of various types, advertising, and public relations may offer a fertile field for local economic development activity. Business services has been a rapidly growing sector of the U.S. economy for several decades, and there is every reason to believe that this growth will continue. Like retailing, business service growth is driven primarily by the presence of a nearby mass of potential customers. A common suburban sequence is for business service growth to occur fairly late in the process. It is preceded by growth in retailing and wholesaling, manufacturing, and perhaps corporate headquarters. When the suburban economy develops sufficient mass, it begins attracting a significant amount of business service activity, frequently in large measure from the central city of the region. It is doubtful that a local development agency can attract much business service activity before its time. But once the critical mass of other economic activity is present, it can be pursued.

Manufacturing is still the number-one target for recruitment by local economic development agencies. Though one hears much about the "post industrial" age, manufacturing is far from dead. At present manufacturing accounts for about 15 percent of U.S. employment and about 25 percent of value added in the U.S. economy. Wages in manufacturing, as the comparison of these two percentages suggests, are well above the national average. Some manufacturing is closely tied to the location of customers because of transport costs or perishability. Cement and bakery products, for example, are so tied. However, many manufactured products are sold to regional, national, or world markets and are thus "footloose." Some types of manufacturing are tied to particular labor markets. The manufacture of genetically engineered products would be an example. But many types of manufacturing are not. The skills required to produce, say, sheet metal office equipment such as file cabinets are quite widely dispersed in the United States. Not only is manufacturing important in its own right, but strength in manufacturing often leads to strength in other areas, such as business services and finance, a point that is made very convincingly in *Manufacturing Matters*.[9]

It is hard to generalize about the place characteristics required to attract manufacturing activity because of the diversity of manufacturing. One way to begin thinking about the community's ability to retain and attract manufacturing is to get an overview of the field. The best source for this purpose is the *Annual Survey of Manufactures*.[10] This will provide information on total employment, capital expenditures, labor cost, purchases of energy and fuel, and several other statistics down to the four-digit level, a total of between 400 and 500 different manufacturing categories.

The overview one gets from the *Annual Survey* and one's own general knowledge can be supplemented by looking at trade journals. Virtually every area of manufacturing will be covered by one or more journals. These will provide an up-to-date picture of what is going on in the field—growth areas, lagging areas, labor issues, international competition, environmental problems, and so on. One tends not to be aware of the existence of trade magazines because they are not sold on newsstands and there generally is not much reason for reading one if one is not in the industry. But they can be a mine of information for the economic developer. If it appears that one's area with its good trucking access, moderate land and labor costs, and proximity to a major metropolitan area might be a good location for bottling plants, then a little time looking through *Beverage World, Beverage Industry,* or *Mid-Continent Bottler* might be a good idea. If plastics forming or fabrication looks as if it might have potential, then one might look into *Plastics Distributor, Modern Plastics, Plastics News,* or *Plastics World.* And so on.

If one wants a picture of interindustry linkages within manufacturing, an input/output table for the U.S. economy might be enlightening. The table lists each sector as both a consumer of inputs from other sectors and as a producer of outputs to other sectors. Thus, if one wants to see how many cents' worth of coke it takes to make a dollar's worth of steel, one can look it up in the table. Similarly, if one wants to see how much of the steel industry's output is sold to the cement industry, one can look that up. In short, one can use the table to see what industries might have a natural affinity, either as customers or as suppliers, for the community's existing industrial structure.[11] This approach is not for every economic development agency, but for the larger agency that is determined to make a fairly serious effort at targeting. As indicated earlier, this is a relatively small minority of all agencies.

As a final step in the assessment of economic development potential, one ought to compare the results of one's thinking with current reality. The process suggested so far has been one of comparing the community with the characteristics of various types of economic activity to see whether there is a good match. As argued before, a great deal of business decision making has personal and other idiosyncratic elements. Therefore the best possible analysis will not correspond entirely to what is happening. On the other hand, if there is an enormous gulf between analysis and reality, then perhaps the analysis should be questioned. Statistics on employment by sector are readily available from state labor departments, but less aggregated data should also be examined. Specifically, individual moves by firms, both in and out, should be considered. Opinions of businessmen, bankers, and brokers who deal in commercial real estate should be solicited. If one grants that most growth is likely to come from the existing economic base, then finding out why firms leave may be just as important as finding out why firms move in.

NOTES

1. There is a large body of location theory, developed over many years and presented by a number of writers, including William Alonso, Walter Isaard, and August Losch. Much of it is quite elegant mathematically, and its use requires a substantial amount of staff time and technical sophistication. In this writer's view, elaborate studies of accessibility are not cost effective for most development agencies. For more formal approaches to accessibility, see Barry M. Moriarty and David J. Cowen, eds., *Industrial Location and Community Development*, University of North Carolina Press, Chapel Hill, 1980. A practical grasp of the rudiments of location may be helpful. See William Alonso, "Location Theory," in *Regional Development and Planning: A Reader*, John Friedman and William Alonso, eds., MIT Press, Cambridge, Mass., 1964. The same article can also be found in *Readings in Urban Economics*, Matthew Edel and Jerome Rothenberg, eds., Macmillan, New York, 1972.

2. For a review of older literature, see George A. Reigeluth, and Harold Wolman, "The Determinants and Implications of Communities' Changing Competitive Advantage: A Review of Literature," Urban Institute, Washington, D.C., 1979,

paper no. 1264-03. A widely cited work on industrial location is Roger W. Schmenner, *Making Business Location Decisions*, Prentice-Hall, Englewood Cliffs, N.J., 1982. Two more recent articles are Gordon D. Hack, "Location Trends: 1958–88," *Area Development*, October 1988, p. 12; and Dennis S. Tosh, Troy A. Fester-vard, and James R. Lumpkin, "Industrial Site Selection Criteria: Are Economic Developers, Manufacturers and Real Estate Brokers Operating on the Same Wave-length," *Economic Development Review*, Fall 1988 (Vol. 6, no. 3), pp. 62–67.

3. Bureau of Labor Statistics, *Area Wage Surveys*, U.S. Department of Labor, Washington, D.C. In general, labor market areas are surveyed on a three-year cycle, with different places surveyed at different points in the cycle. Thus, some standardizing has to be done to get data for comparable places surveyed at different times.

4. Bureau of Labor Statistics, *Employment and Earnings*, U.S. Department of Labor, Washington, D.C.

5. Some caution should be advised here. As a rule of thumb, recipients are about half of the total unemployed and may not represent an entirely random sample of the unemployed. This may be especially true in periods of prolonged unemployment when some of the unemployed exhaust their benefits and drop off the list of recipients without leaving the ranks of the unemployed.

6. Uniform statistics on a variety of offenses are available from the Federal Bureau of Investigation, Washington, D.C.

7. National data on energy costs can be obtained from *Monthly Energy Review*, Department of Energy, Washington, D.C.

8. *Means Construction Indexes*, R.S. Means Co., Duxbury, Mass., and *Dodge Building Cost Calculator and Valuation Guide*, McGraw-Hill, New York.

9. Stephen S. Cohen and John Zysman, *Manufacturing Matters: The Myth of the Post-Industrial Economy*, Basic Books, New York, 1987.

10. *Annual Survey of Manufactures*, Bureau of the Census, U.S. Department of Commerce, Washington, D.C.

11. An eighty-five-sector model can be found in the May 1984 issue of *Survey of Current Business*, Bureau of Economic Analysis, U.S. Department of Commerce. Newer and larger tables might be obtained from the BEA, from the economics department of a major bank or university, or from an economic consulting firm.

10

Development Planning

Few economic developers will be called upon to do detailed site planning.[1] That is work done most commonly by planning or engineering consultants. However, the economic developer sometimes does, and more often should, participate in the community's overall planning process. This chapter is provided as background for such participation.

A primary goal of the economic developer is to assure that an adequate supply of land is set aside for industrial and commercial development in the foreseeable future. It is also important to assure that land-use controls are reasonable and that land-use plans do not contain within them the seeds of future opposition to commercial and industrial development.

The three planning instruments to which the economic developer should pay particular attention are the master plan, the zoning ordinance, and the long-term capital budget.[2] The master plan lays out the overall pattern of land uses and infrastructure development. It shows where the main blocks of residential, commercial, and industrial land will be, as well as the overall pattern of roads, infrastructure such as water and sewer lines, and public facilities. It is the long-term vision of the physical future of the municipality.

The zoning ordinance and the map that accompanies it show the type and the intensity of development permitted on every parcel of land in the municipality. It specifies type of use, coverage ratios, setbacks, maximum building heights, parking requirements, and the like.

In a competently done planning process the master plan and the zoning ordinance are closely related. The ordinance is a detailed expression of the broader vision expressed in the master plan.

The long-term capital budget is the schedule by which the municipality plans to provide the infrastructure, in the form of roads, bridges, water and sewer lines, parking facilities, public buildings, and the like, that will help to bring about the vision embodied in the master plan.

The particular interest of the economic developer in the planning process is to see that adequate amounts of developable land are provided for and supplied with adequate utilities and access. A related interest is to see that the pattern of land-use and infrastructure development planning does not sow the seeds of future conflict over land use.

In the short term the zoning ordinance is likely to be the item of most concern to the economic developer because it is the item over which conflict and litigation are most likely to arise. In the very long term, the capital budget may be most important, for capital expenditures, particularly roads and utilities, generate economic forces. And these, in the long term, cause plans and ordinances to change. An ordinance can be amended or revoked. But concrete lasts for a long time.

ESTIMATING LAND NEEDS

The place to begin thinking about land needs for industry and commerce is with the floor space requirements per worker for different types of activity. From such figures, acreage requirements for likely levels of employment can be estimated. Such estimates are necessarily rough ones, but they can still be highly useful for planning purposes. Table 10.1 shows figures that can be used as starting points.

These figures are guidelines only, and large variations may occur within categories. For example, electronics assembly or garment manufacturing, where the product is not bulky and workers sit almost shoulder to shoulder, might average under 200 square feet per worker, while assembly of sheet-metal ductwork for heating and air-conditioning systems might average well over 500 square feet per worker. Yet all fall in the light-manufacturing category.

The coverage ratio—the ratio between floor area and land area—is subject to considerable variation due to differences in degree of urbanization, land costs, and land-use controls. A substantial percentage of commercially used land is devoted to parking. Here, too, variations are great, depending upon the variables listed above as well as upon the availability of public transportation. A parking-area-to-floor-area ratio adequate for a downtown department store might spell economic disaster for a suburban shopping center five miles away.

As an example of estimating work force per acre, consider light manufacturing in an industrial park setting in a suburban or nonmetropolitan area. One-story construction is assumed. Where land values are low, the one-story manufacturing structure is favored for a number of reasons. Lighter construction is possible. Interior space is not lost to stairwells and elevator

Table 10.1
Gross Floor Space Requirements

Activity	Gross Square Footage per Employee
Retailing	500
Wholesaling and warehousing	1,000
Light manufacturing	500
Heavy manufacturing	1,000
Office activities	250
Research and development	500

Sources: Joseph D. Chiara and Lee Koppleman, *Planning Design Criteria,* Van Nostrand & Reinhold, New York, 1969; Donald C. Lochmoeller et al., *Industrial Development Handbook,* Urban Land Institute, Washington, D.C., 1975; Travel and Facilities Section, Transportation Planning Division, Arizona Department of Transportation, in cooperation with U.S. Department of Transportation, *Trip Generation Intensity Factors,* Federal Highway Administration, Washington, D.C., 1976; John M. Levy et al., *Commercial and Public Construction in Westchester County,* Westchester County Department of Planning, White Plains, N.Y., 1974.

shafts. Materials handling is often more efficient and the layout is more amenable to straight-through processes. If an area is not highly urbanized, most of the work force will arrive by car. An allowance of 0.8 parking spaces per employee would be reasonable. Typically, parking areas without parking attendants require 350 to 400 square feet per car, about half for spaces and half for circulation. If we allow 500 square feet of floor space per worker, total land coverage per worker is now up to 850 to 900 square feet. If a reasonable allowance is made for truck loading and visitor parking, this figure might rise to 1,000 square feet. Not all of an industrial park site can be used. Land-use controls will call for some buffering space. Topographic, drainage, or other physical problems may further reduce usable area. If we assume, somewhat conservatively, that only 50 percent of the average industrial park site will be usable, then the land area per worker rises to 2,000 square feet, yielding a figure of 22 workers per acre.

There is obviously no way to predict employee density precisely, but the figure will serve for rough planning purposes. Comparable calculations can be made for other types of activity. For corporate headquarters in the suburbs, employee density might be placed at one worker per 300 gross square feet and parking requirements at three spaces per 1,000 square feet. Assuming a one-story structure and no structured parking, about 600 square feet per worker are required for floor space and parking area. Assuming 50 percent site utilization, this would suggest about 36 workers per acre.

Since parking requirements are a major factor in land requirements, standards for a number of types of activity are shown in Table 10.2. Note that these are all given for situations in which space is not a major constraint. High densities of development, the existence of heavily utilized public transportation, and high land costs will all force these figures down. As land costs rise from being measured in cents per square foot to dollars per square foot, multistory construction becomes economical for many types of commercial use. Manufacturing, however, is not likely to be one of these uses. Where land costs are so high as to mandate multistory construction, manufacturing activity is not likely to develop.

Table 10.2
Parking Requirements for Various Types of Activities

Activity	Spaces per 1,000 Gross Square Feet*
Light manufacturing	2
Heavy industry	1
Corporate headquarters and other office activities	3
Wholesaling and warehousing	1
Regional shopping center	4
Neighborhood shopping center	2

*Assumes suburban density of development and relatively low utilization of public transportation.

Sources: Joseph D. Chiara and Lee Koppleman, *Planning Design Criteria*, Van Nostrand & Reinhold, New York, 1969; and Donald C. Lochmoeller et al., *Industrial Development Handbook*, Urban Land Institute, Washington, D.C., 1975. Observations and estimates are by the author.

In estimating land requirements per worker, several cautions should be observed. In general, it is best to make assumptions on the basis of recent density of development. Observe what has been done and sold recently; no better guide to marketability can be found. Do not lean too heavily on existing zoning ordinances in making such estimates. Where zoning specifies unrealistically low densities, the economic forces for rezoning and/or the granting of variances are very powerful. So, too, may be the legal forces. On the other hand, the zoning ordinance may, on occasion, permit densities of development that practice and technology will not sustain. Zoning puts a ceiling on density but does not compel construction at that density. For example, assume a zoning ordinance in a suburban area specifies a maximum floor-area ratio (FAR) of 0.8 for light manufacturing. The chances that anyone will build to this density are remote. There is, as noted above, a strong preference for single-story plants. Parking, circulation, and truck unloading space will probably require as much square footage per worker as will the building itself. We are thus down to an FAR of 0.5. Given some loss of space for buffering and setback requirements, the probable FAR drops still further. In modern suburban light-manufacturing development, an FAR of 0.2 or 0.3 is a reasonable estimate. It is rare that any sizable area develops to the maximum permitted by zoning.

Do not expect new development to be more dense than existing development unless there is some convincing reason for it that can be pointed to. In 1950 there were four Americans for every automobile. There are now fewer than two Americans per automobile. This alone should make one wary of expecting new development to be denser than the average for the present inventory.

It should also be understood that not all land apparently available for development will be developed. Initial development may leave behind parcels of small size or unsuitable geometry. Environmental or other unanticipated problems may arise. The market for industrial and commercial space may change. In short, space requirements should be estimated realistically and generously.

Beyond simply assuring adequate acreage, some specific points need to be considered:

- Development cost rises with steepness of grade. As a rule of thumb, slopes over 5 percent should be regarded as relatively unlikely to be developed. (In urban areas, one can find both residential and commercial development on much steeper slopes. But this is often a residual from the days when a different transportation technology and land-use pattern placed a much greater emphasis on centrality.) Industrial land should be well drained and outside the floodplain. It also should not be located so that its development poses significant environmental problems. If it does, community opposition and litigation can be anticipated when the time for development approaches.

- Land earmarked for industrial development should be relatively free of obstacles to construction, such as rock outcroppings, whose presence will push up construction costs. Subsoil conditions should be suitable for construction without excessive preparation costs. High shrink/swell potential or the necessity for driving piles will push up construction costs and render the land less competitive with other sites.

- Site geometry is important. A parcel 250 feet by 1,600 feet holds far less industrial potential than a parcel 500 feet by 800 feet, when all other conditions are equal. The latter parcel can be developed with fewer feet of internal roadway and less expenditure on utility lines; it has a shorter periphery, which minimizes land lost for buffering and setbacks. The greater depth will permit building and loading area shapes that cannot be accommodated on the shallower parcel. Thus, a land inventory composed of many small or oddly shaped pieces may hold a great deal less potential than the simple addition of acreage will suggest. Large blocks of land with sufficient depth are highly desirable. Industry requirements vary tremendously. Chapin and Kaiser quote 1,000 feet as a desirable minimum depth for a rail-served site (the ideal configuration being a site located between parallel rail and highway rights-of-way). This is essentially a heavy-industry criterion, as indicated by the term "rail served." For highway-served sites (generally meaning light industry), they quote a minimum depth of 600 to 800 feet. These numbers are not binding, and one can see successful development in many urban areas where they are not met. Nonetheless, if they can be achieved, the chance of seeing development take place is enhanced.

- Availability of utilities is an obvious consideration. Water, sewer, and adequate electric service are vital. Natural gas service is desirable, although, as noted earlier, it does not enjoy nearly as large a cost advantage over petroleum at this writing as it did in the 1970s and early 1980s.

- Adequate access is essential. What constitutes adequate access varies by industry. For corporate headquarters, automobile access is primary. For a wholesaler, being close to a good truck route is likely to be the predominant consideration. Some manufacturers will be concerned only with highway access. Others will regard rail access as being desirable or essential.

In many instances, it is desirable to achieve some separation between commercial and other traffic for the sake of minimizing community opposition to development. Additional traffic is often the number-one reason for community opposition to commercial and industrial development. The writer witnessed the sudden death of an industrial park proposal in a community that needed it very badly when it became apparent to the politically popular legislator of an adjacent community that a small number of trucks would travel for several hundred yards through a lightly populated part of her community. The objection seemed trivial to the writer and a number of others, but overwhelming to the legislator. The site has been growing weeds every since.

Future traffic capacity is also a factor to be considered. In general, one cannot expect a community to pay for lane miles of roadway years in advance of the time they will be needed. On the other hand, traffic generation from industrially and commercially zoned land can be estimated and rights-of-way can be reserved. Peak-hour volumes (the critical figure in most cases) can be estimated. For most agglomerations of activities, the peak hours are the morning and evening rush hours, with volume in the evening peak generally somewhat higher. For particular activities, however, the peak hour may not coincide with the general peak. For example, the retailing peak hour generally occurs in the afternoon before the evening rush hour begins. Table 10.3 shows average peak-hour/trip-generation figures for a number of activities. Much more detailed information can be obtained from the traffic engineering literature, including the document cited in Table 10.3.

The reader will note the ratios between the per-employee and the per-

1,000-square-feet figures have implicit in them floor space per worker and that these implicit figures correspond approximately to those of Table 10.1.

From peak-hour figures, the adequacy of the existing or proposed road network can be estimated. Making such estimates is a technical matter best left to the traffic engineer. To provide a rough number for thinking about capacity, a modern freeway, under ideal conditions, might achieve a volume of 2,000 cars per lane per hour.[3] Frequent interchanges, grades, curves, reduced sight distances, and trucking all lower this figure. In general, a two-way, two-lane road, with passing permitted in both directions, has no more total capacity than a single comparable lane in one direction would have. Intersections reduce roadway capacity, as do merging or exiting points. Strip development reduces highway capacity in the latter manner. One might think of it as introducing turbulence into the traffic stream, much as scale inside a pipe introduces turbulence into the flow of water.

Table 10.3
Peak-Hour Trip Generation for Various Types of Activities

Activity	1,000 Gross Sq. Ft.	Peak-Hour Trips by Employee
Industrial parks	.8	.5
Large shopping centers	2.3	1.1
Offices	2.5	.6
Warehouses	1.0	.9
Large free-standing factories	.8	.4
Small free-standing factories	1.2	.5
Research and development facilities	1.2	.6

Source: Travel and Facilities Section, Transportation Planning Division, Arizona Department of Transportation, in cooperation with U.S. Department of Transportation, *Trip Generation Intensity Factors*, Federal Highway Administration, Washington, D.C., 1976.

It would be naive to argue that adequate road capacity must always be present for development to occur. In many cases the congestion caused by development provides the pressure to increase road capacity. Then, too, there is often more give in the system than initial estimates suggest. For example, when peak-hour congestion becomes a serious problem, firms may begin staggering work hours. In addition, some nonbusiness traffic may be shifted to nonpeak hours. A road that is at capacity in the peak hour may accommodate still more traffic as congestion spreads the peak over more time. Nonetheless, to the extent possible, it is worthwhile for the economic developer to press the case for providing adequate capacity. If nothing else, he or she can urge that the option to provide future capacity not be fore-closed. Congestion costs are a major deterrent to attracting industry. But beyond this direct effort, congestion generates an anti-development, anti-growth sentiment.

The importance of public transportation is hard to predict. Public transit use in the United States peaked in 1945 and declined sharply for several decades thereafter. In the 1970s and early 1980s there was a slight rebound due primarily to increased federal funding and the completion or expansion of several systems. In general, per capita automobile ownership in the United States continued to rise during the 1980s and the dispersion of people and employment continued. This does not bode well for the future of public transportation. It is possible that increases in energy costs might favor public transportation at some time in the future. After the oil price shocks of 1973–74 and 1978–79, there were some who felt that continued increases in energy costs would favor a revival of public transportation. However, energy prices declined and today, in real terms, are slightly lower than they were in 1973. Whether concern with climatic change will some-day cause the United States to raise the prices of fossil fuels such as petro-leum remains to be seen. Should energy costs rise substantially, one effect might be to favor sites served by public transportation. But another effect—one the author suspects is more likely—might be to promote a pattern of dispersed self-sufficiency with residential and a variety of synergistic com-mercial and industrial uses in close physical proximity. At this point it is very difficult to feel confident in discussing the future importance of public transportation.

LAND-USE CONTROLS

Since the inception of zoning about the time of World War I, it has been understood that residential areas should be protected from industry for ob-vious and unarguable reasons.[4] It took several decades to realize that there are strong, though less obvious, reasons for seeking to exclude residential uses from industrial areas.

One reason is to prevent the breakup of large parcels. Large parcels can always be subdivided for small industrial and commercial users if that is what market forces dictate. However, if large parcels are broken up by scat-tered residential development, some industrial and commercial opportuni-ties are permanently lost. But perhaps a more important reason for the prohibition of residential development in commercial and industrial zones is a political one. By permitting residential development (or some types of public development) in a commercial or industrial zone, a predictably anti-development constituency is created. The fact that someone buys or rents a house in an area, knowing its predominant zoning is industrial, does not prevent him or her from opposing subsequent development on the grounds that it intrudes upon his or her tranquillity or lowers the value of his or her investment. This phenomenon has been noted, in particular, in connection with airports. Populations that have moved in after the airport was in operation have often exerted strenuous pressures to reduce or at least block the expansion of airport activity. Rather than becoming involved in after-the-fact conflict, it is better to avoid conflict by zoning in such a manner that the problem does not arise.

Just as industrial land merits protection from residential development, so it may merit protection from other types of commercial development. Scattered retail development may chop up a large site that had much more long-term potential for industrial or other commercial use.

Reasonableness in zoning is important, though the term cannot be defined with precision. To the writer, it implies some compromise between the needs of commerce and industry, on one hand, and legitimate community goals, on the other. The writer tends to favor performance standards over rigid categories, as do many planners. Rather than zoning out warehousing because it may involve excessive truck traffic, why not define permitted uses in terms of vehicle trips? Rather than banning machine shops because of their potential for noise, why not cast part of the ordinance in terms of decibels?

In adopting an ordinance, it is very easy to include requirements that do not confer great benefits on the community but do impose substantial costs on users. Many, if not most, zoning ordinances are adaptations of other ordinances. Few are written de novo. The planning consultant who turns out zoning ordinances for client communities is likely to do a certain amount on an off-the-shelf basis and realize some economies of scale in their production. Then, too, there is often a tendency to lean in the direction of restrictiveness simply because it is to the community that the draft ordinance is submitted for approval. Because the land-value reduction caused by zoning is not a cost borne by the community, there is little motivation to ascertain that the public benefits equal the private costs.

An unduly low coverage requirement may make some types of commercial development uneconomic. Assume that land zoned for and suitable for warehousing sells for $2 per square foot. If the maximum FAR permitted for this use is lowered from 40 percent to 20 percent, the land cost per square foot of floor space rises from $5 to $10. Warehouses have relatively low construction costs. If the per-square-foot cost of construction is $25, then the combined construction and land cost has risen from $30 to $35. That 17 percent increase may be enough to cause wholesalers, who are somewhat footloose, to locate elsewhere.

If the lower coverage requirement really serves community purposes, then perhaps it is worth the lost tax revenues and jobs. But because the act of zoning itself costs the municipality nothing, one should make an effort to see that the zoning process does not achieve small community benefits at the price of large, but not immediately evident, community or private costs.[5] Similar comments might be made with regard to other aspects of zoning, such as setback and screening requirements, parking requirements, height and bulk requirements, and lists of permitted and nonpermitted uses. The question is whether requirements meet real community needs (which they often do), or whether some of them are there because they are in the ordinance from which the later ordinance was copied, or in a more general sense, because they have no explicit cost to the community.

Particularly in suburban areas, there often is a community preference for low coverage ratios (low FARs). This is understandable because low ratios imply smaller impacts upon both the particular parcel of land itself and the immediate environs. There may, however, be a price to be paid at least in two respects. First, there may result a more scattered pattern of development that generates increased vehicular traffic and eats up potential open space. Site impact is minimized but community or regional impact is not. Second, there is the possibility that where usable commercial land is limited, excessive coverage requirements will exact a price from the community later on. The corporate headquarters that employs 1,200 on a 100-acre tract with an FAR of 0.07 (calculated from a ratio of 250 gross square feet per employee) may be extremely attractive to the community. It offers a revenue/ cost surplus and preserves a substantial amount of green space at no public cost. In the long term, however, the exchange of a very large block of prime commercial land for a relatively small number of jobs may be regretted.

In the writer's decade in planning and economic development, he has never heard a community object to industrial or commercial development on the grounds of not being dense enough. But if developable land, in sufficiently large parcels with suitable geometry, is one of the community's prime economic assets, perhaps this apparently inevitable preference for low density is a form of municipal myopia.

In 1951 the National Industrial Zoning Committee established eleven principles of industrial zoning, which are worth quoting here:[6]

1. Most communities require a certain amount of industrial development to produce a sound economy.

2. Zoning controls are basic tools in the reservation of space for industry; guidance of industrial location into a desirable pattern; and, provision of related facilities and areas needed for convenient and balanced economy.

3. Industrial use is a legitimate land use possessing integrity comparable to other classes of land use established under zoning and is entitled to protection against encroachment.

4. Through proper zoning, industrial and residential areas can be good neighbors.

5. Industry will continue to grow and most industries will require larger areas in the future. There is need for a reclassification of industry based on modern

manufacturing processes and the prevailing policy of plant construction in order to determine the desirability for inclusion in a given area.

6. Industrial potentialities of lands bearing a favorable relationship to transportation should be recognized in the zoning process.

7. Industrial zoning and highway planning should go hand in hand.

8. Special consideration should be given to the street layout in industrial areas.

9. Zoning ordinances should be permissive rather than prohibitive.

10. A good zoning ordinance should be sufficiently definite to convey to a landowner a clear concept of what he can do with his land.

11. Industrial zoning can be most effective when considered on a metropolitan basis.

Perhaps the most difficult question is how much land to reserve for industrial and commercial use. Chiara and Koppleman suggest planning for a fifty-year horizon, but obviously any number one might name is an arbitrary figure.[7] How much employment growth to expect within a given period is another question. If there is some consensus about the future of population growth, inferences can then be made regarding employment. Nationally, there are about 45 people in the work force for every 100 of population, a ratio that is probably good enough for rough approximations. But it must be noted that population projection is far from a science. Looking at old population estimates in the light of current data is not usually a confidence-inspiring experience.

Land-use requirements should be estimated generously. Not all the land designated for industrial uses will inevitably be used for such purposes. Competition from residential, public, or conservation uses may claim part of the inventory of commercial and industrial land. In particular, the competition from residential uses may prove overwhelming if the site in question has attractive aspects such as water access. Questions of site geometry or subsoil conditions may also reduce the amount of land actually available for economic development.

Finally, the market demand for commercial and industrial land has changed before and may well change again. Production technologies, the mix of business and industry, changes in the pattern of residential location, and changes in transportation and communications technology have altered the demand for industrial and commercial land in the past. There is no reason to believe that the current pattern is any more permanent than past patterns. The economic developer generally confronts a buyer's market. Many firms have some degree of footlooseness, and the number of firms seeking to relocate is vastly smaller than the number of communities seeking new firms. If the community does not have what the firm is seeking, the firm is more likely to choose another community than to adjust its wants.

How much public participation there should be in the provision of sites above and beyond the planning and community capital budgeting matters previously discussed is a difficult question. If there is clear demand for sites in the community but the private sector is not able to assemble marketable sites, then there is clear need for public participation. Public powers of eminent domain may be used for site assembly and sites may be marketed below cost. If the private sector is able to produce marketable sites, then the case for public action is weaker. The survey cited earlier did not suggest that a large percentage of economic developers viewed site assembly and preparation as a highly productive activity. On the other hand, many communities do it and many state development agencies view it as highly important.

For example, the central effort of Virginia's state economic development agency is to encourage communities to develop an inventory of marketable sites. State economic development officials spend a large part of their professional time assisting and encouraging communities to acquire land (or options to land), to provide suitable infrastructure, and, in many cases, to construct shell buildings. Both state and community officials can cite numerous instances of firms that were attracted because sites or structures were quickly available. To some extent, the fact that one community invests public funds in site development forces other communities to do the same because public funds lower the cost of sites.

Both the Economic Development Administration and HUD's Urban Development Action Grant program (both of which were discussed at some length in the first edition of this book) were predicated on the assumption that publicly developed sites available at reduced costs would give aided communities a significant advantage in attracting investment. Whether or not this assumption was correct is arguable. In their heyday, when each program was funded at about $0.5 billion annually, their total still amounted to less than 0.1 percent of GNP. Thus, determining whether they made much change in the overall pattern of economic location is difficult.

On balance, this writer is generally skeptical about the need for public investment in sites in the majority of communities. However, the reader should be aware that many competent economic developers take the opposite view.

NOTES

1. For an introduction to site planning, see Michael D. Breyard et al., *Business and Industrial Park Development Handbook*, The Urban Land Institute, Washington, D.C., 1988. For a more general work on physical planning, see F. Stuart Chapin and Edward J. Kaiser, *Urban Land Use Planning*, University of Illinois Press, Urbana, 1979.

2. A nontechnical overview of the community planning process, as well as refer-

ences to more technical literature, can be found in John M. Levy, *Contemporary Urban Planning*, Prentice-Hall, Englewood Cliffs, N.J., 1988.

3. Maximum flow is achieved at about 35 mph. Above that speed the increased spacing between vehicles compensates for the higher speed.

4. Many older zoning ordinances are written in a pyramidal form. The highest use is permitted in any zone and each succeeding use is permitted in the first zone that allows it, plus every lower zone. Thus, if the highest-use zone, as is common, is single-family housing, that use is permitted everywhere. If the second-highest-use zone is apartments, that use is permitted everywhere except in single-family zones. If the lowest-use zone is heavy industry, that use is permitted only in the heavy-industry zone. The illustration is somewhat simplified in that each of the uses cited above is likely to be broken down into a number of subcategories. Since residential uses are considered higher uses, such an ordinance protects designated residential areas from commercial intrusion but does not protect commercial areas from residential intrusion.

5. This theme is explored in detail in William A. Fischel, *The Economics of Zoning Laws: A Property Rights Approach*, Johns Hopkins University Press, Baltimore, 1985.

6. Quoted from Donald C. Lochmoeller et al., *Industrial Development Handbook*, Urban Land Institute, Washington, D.C., 1979.

7. Joseph D. Chiara and Lee Koppleman, *Planning Design Criteria*, Van Nostrand & Reinhold, New York, 1969.'

11

Development Financing

It is important for the economic developer to have some knowledge of finance. In some cases the economic developer will participate directly in the details of structuring financial arrangements. More commonly, he or she will leave those details to others. However, it is still important to understand both what is being done and the range of options. This chapter will presume that the reader has some general background in finance, perhaps as much as could be gathered by spending several hours reading a book on real estate finance. For the reader who is considering the practice of economic development but has no such background, such reading would be time well spent. But one caveat is necessary here. Given the rate at which the field changes, it is not possible to keep up by reading books. Laws and regulations change frequently, and the combination of large sums of money and large numbers of agile minds guarantees that new tricks of the trade will appear with considerable frequency. The economic developer who would like to keep current would be well advised to read some periodicals such as *Real Estate Review* and *National Real Estate Investor.*

We begin with a few general comments on conventional financing sources. After that we turn to the Tax Reform Act of 1986 and the very substantial changes that it has wrought in the field of real estate and development financing.[1] We then proceed to a discussion of a variety of financing assistance programs available to economic developers. Some very brief references are made to older programs that have been discontinued or are much reduced in scope. These, including EDA, UDAG, CETA, and IRBs, are described in some detail in the first edition of this book and in much of the older economic development literature.

CONVENTIONAL SOURCES OF FUNDING

In many cases the developer will use one or more sources for short-term financing and one or more other sources for long-term financing. In some cases there may also be a "gap" financing between the two. A very common source of short-term financing is the commercial bank. The bank will lend for the construction phase with the understanding that when this phase is complete, the developer will obtain permanent financing with which the bank will be repaid. In fact, the bank generally will not lend at all unless the developer has in hand a commitment for permanent financing, a "takeout" commitment. In general, banks will not lend more than 70 or 80 percent of the total project cost. By insisting that there be a substantial amount of investor equity, the lender protects its own interest. The owner's large stake gives the owner powerful motivation to see that the project succeeds. Then, too, if the lender's exposure is limited to, say, 70 percent, the market value can decline by 30 percent before the remaining value of the project falls below the debt owed to the lender. In general, the riskier the project, the less the exposure that the lender will accept. Parenthetically, we might note that in 1988 and 1989, when the details of the Savings and Loan (S&L) disaster began to emerge, cases in which the owner's equity was extremely low, and even some cases in which loans exceeded project value, figured prominently.

Permanent financing comes from a variety of sources. Insurance companies and pension funds have large sums to invest and hold many billions in commercial mortgages. Commercial real estate, while not quite as safe as government paper, tends to be a reasonably safe investment for institutions that, by virtue of their fiduciary responsibilities, need to invest in a prudent manner. In recent years, the deregulation of S&L institutions has permitted them to invest heavily in commercial real estate. However, the recent excesses of the S&L industry have brought about reregulation and it is not now possible to say what the role of S&Ls will be in the years to come.

Real Estate investment trusts (REITs) have been a major factor in the financing of commercial real estate in the 1980s. Basically, a REIT is a corporation that, because of particular provisions of the IRS code, is able to avoid the usual double taxation of corporate income. Normally a corporation pays taxes on its profits in the form of a corporate income tax. When the profits are distributed to the shareholders, they are again taxed, this time as personal income. The REIT, however, pays no corporate income tax. To be classified as a REIT, the organization must meet various requirements. One is that it have more than 100 stockholders and that the 5 largest stockholders must own no more than 50 percent of the stock. The REIT must invest the major share of its funds in real estate, and it must distribute at least 95 percent of its profits at the end of each fiscal year. There are numerous types of REITs. Mortgage REITs specialize in investment in mortgages. Equity REITs specialize in equity (partial ownership of properties) rather than in holding debt. Within each of these broad classifications are various subtypes. The REIT permits the individual who wishes to invest in real estate to do so with the same ease that he or she could invest in stocks or bonds. The investor simply buys a security but assumes no operating or managerial responsibility. In that sense, REITs have served to bring substantial amounts of capital into real estate that might otherwise have gone into other security markets.

A variation on the REIT theme is the Real Estate Mortgage Investment Conduit (REMIC) authorized under the 1986 Tax Reform Act. The REMIC can issue a wide variety of securities or types of interests secured by mortgages. This flexibility may give the REMIC some advantages over the REIT. A property owner, for example, might transfer a property to a REMIC in return for some type of interest in the REMIC without being subject to capital gains tax at the time.[2] REITs and REMICs are essentially creatures of the tax code that owe their advantages to the avoidance of double taxation, a variety of other tax advantages, and their access to the equity markets.

With the growth of world trade and the U.S. trade deficit of the 1980s, foreign financing of U.S. real estate development has assumed considerable importance. Numerous European and Japanese banks invest heavily in U.S. real estate, both through ownership and through the purchase of mortgages. For the large and sophisticated U.S. investor there also exists the option of borrowing in other currencies for the purchase of U.S. real estate. For many years real interest rates in both Japan and some European nations, including West Germany, have been lower than in the United States, and therein lies the advantage of borrowing in another currency. The risk is that a fall in the value of the dollar against the borrowed currency will impose a loss upon the borrower.[3] Clearly this is not a strategy for the unsophisticated or risk-averse investor.

CHANGES IN REAL ESTATE FINANCE SINCE 1986

As noted, changes in the tax code made by the Tax Reform Act of 1986 have drastically changed real estate investment. The general compromise embodied in the act was to reduce marginal tax rates but to render this reduction more or less "revenue neutral" by expanding the tax base. It was argued that these changes would foster economic growth in two ways. The lower marginal rates would increase the motivation of entrepreneurs and investors, and the elimination of tax shelters would eliminate distortions in the pattern of investment. Investors would focus more on the productivity of an investment and less on its tax treatment. Four important changes are the following:

1. Reduction in the maximum marginal tax rate for individuals

2. Treatment of capital gains as ordinary income
3. Limitation of passive losses
4. Stretching out of depreciation (cost-recovery) schedules.

When Ronald Reagan assumed office in 1981, the maximum tax rate on individual income was 70 percent. This was subsequently cut to 50 percent and then, in 1986, to 27.5 percent. For wealthy individuals the value of a tax loss was thus cut by more than half. In 1980, for the wealthiest individual, a tax loss of $1 increased after-tax income by 70 cents. After 1986 a tax loss of $1 increased after-tax income by only 27.5 cents.

Prior to 1986, 60 percent of a capital gain was exempt from taxation. The remaining 40 percent was taxed as ordinary income. Thus a dollar of income obtained through capital gains left a high-bracket recipient with considerably more after-tax income than did a dollar of earned income. For example, $1 of earned income in the 50 percent bracket left the recipient with 50 cents after-tax income. But $1 of capital gain left the same individual with 80 cents of after-tax income. (The tax would be 50 percent of the 40 cents subject to tax.) Since 1986 capital gains have been treated as ordinary income, and thus taxed more heavily.

Another part of the Tax Reform Act was the very sharp limitation of passive losses. A passive loss is one that one takes in an enterprise in which one has no active role. For example, prior to the Tax Reform Act an individual might buy a share in a limited partnership that invested in real estate. The individual's liability was limited to the amount of his or her investment. Losses incurred by the partnership (prorated by the individual's share in the partnership) constituted losses that could be subtracted from the individual's taxable income. The lack of limitations on passive losses, coupled with high marginal tax brackets, made investment in real estate and other syndications attractive to many individuals even when the fundamentals of the investment were not very sound. After the Tax Reform Act individuals with incomes under $250,000 could take only $7,500 in passive losses and individuals with incomes above $250,000 could, in general, not take any passive losses.

The Tax Reform Act of 1986 also stretched out real estate cost-recovery schedules, a point that takes a few words of explanation. If an asset such as a building is used to produce income, it is only fair that the owner of the asset be allowed to deduct from taxable income the wearing out or depreciation of the asset. Otherwise, he or she will be overstating his income and will therefore be overtaxed. In 1981 the depreciation rules (referred to after 1981 as "cost recovery") for commercial property were changed so as to be extremely favorable to real estate investors. Properties could be fully depreciated in only fifteen years. Each year the investor could subtract one-fifteenth of the value of the property from his or her taxable income.[4] This period is much shorter than the actual service life of most commercial real estate, and thus was extremely favorable treatment. For example, assume an investment of $1 million, of which $100,000 was land and $900,000 was structure. The $900,000 could be depreciated in fifteen increments of $60,000 each. For an investor in the 50 percent tax bracket, that meant cumulated tax savings of $450,000, hardly a trivial amount against an investment of $1 million. If one computes the present value of the tax savings, using a discount rate of 10 percent, one gets a figure of $228,182—a smaller but still not a trivial amount. If one assumed that the building had an actual service life of thirty years and computed the present value of straight-line depreciation over thirty years for an investor in the same tax bracket, the present value would be $141,404. The difference between that figure and the previous figure of $228,182 is the "excess depreciation." Thus on a $1 million investment the federal government, for this investor, is providing a tax shelter or tax preference whose present value is $86,778.

It is true that the investor must figure his or her capital gain down to the depreciated value when the building is sold. However, the investor has the use of the money during the time before the sale, and capital gains at that time were treated in a very favorable manner. Then, too, there are ways to obtain cash from a structure without paying capital gains tax—for example, by refinancing it rather than selling it. In 1984 the accelerated cost-recovery period was extended from fifteen to eighteen years. This was not quite so favorable as the fifteen-year period, but was still substantially shorter than the service life of the average commercial building. The Tax Reform Act of 1986 extended the depreciation period for commercial properties to 31.5 years, a period that is a much more realistic measure of the life of a commercial structure. In the end the investor can take as much depreciation as ever. However, because he or she receives it much further in the future, its present value is much smaller.

The combined effect of all of the above changes was to make commercial real estate a different sort of investment and also a somewhat less attractive one. Prior to the Tax Reform Act of 1986, much investment in commercial real estate was driven by tax considerations. Wealthy individuals participated in syndications primarily because of the tax consequences rather than the underlying fundamentals of the investment. The favorable treatment of capital gains and the tax advantages of rapid depreciation led to many investments in circumstances that the prudent investor would avoid. The present real estate investment climate is much more likely to be influenced by the fundamentals of the property in question and less by tax considerations than was formerly the case. The limited partnership, whose essential advantage was that it could deliver excess depreciation and favorable treatment of capital gains to passive investors, appears to have lost much of its appeal. Its place will probably be taken in large measure by REITs and REMICs.

FINANCING ASSISTANCE FROM GOVERNMENT

In this section, a number of commonly used incentive devices are listed. But before discussing them, let us note a very general consideration. All of them exist to lower the cost of capital and thus facilitate development. The use of subsidy is often discussed in terms of lowering the cost of capital sufficiently to make a project show an adequate return. That is valid if the firm is in some way bound to the community. Then the decision is either "go" or "no go," and enough money to push the project across the dividing line between inadequate and adequate return may be sufficient. However, if the firm is footloose, the issue is not one of achieving an adequate return but a maximum return. Even if the footlooseness is confined to a single metropolitan area, the firm may still be in a position to choose among a number of communities offering a variety of assistance packages. It is in the interest of the firm to make the development agency believe that a subsidy will be decisive. It is also in the interest of the firm to make the agency believe that there are many other communities anxious to attract it and willing to offer generous financial incentives in order to do so. Inevitably, the firm knows its own costs, motivations, and other options better than the development agency. Thus, in many, if not most, instances that assistance has been provided, the agency will not be certain that said assistance was decisive.

Most of the descriptions that follow are very general. The variety of incentive programs is enormous. One reason for the variety is that state constitutions vary in their provisions regarding gifts, loans, and other financial relations between state and local governments, on the one hand, and firms and individuals, on the other. Some commonly offered types of financing follow. The list is far from complete.

1. *Tax-exempt financing*. With many types of development assistance, government enjoys the advantage that it can borrow in tax-exempt capital markets. In the late 1970s and early 1980s tax-exempt securities carried about three-fourths the interest rate of comparable taxable securities. For example, if an AAA rated corporate bond carried an interest rate of 10 percent, an industrial revenue bond (IRB) of equal quality might have carried an interest rate in the 7–8 percent range. A general obligation bond issued by local government would carry a slightly lower rate because it is backed by the taxing power of that government. We might note that since the Great Depression defaults by local governments have been virtually unheard of. Thus local general obligation paper is an extremely safe investment, perhaps second only to federal and state paper in safety. Given the reduction in the top marginal tax rate under the Reagan administration, the difference between tax-exempt and taxable rates will shrink. However, the public agency that uses the municipal or state capacity to borrow in tax-exempt markets still enjoys some cost advantage over a conventional lender, such as a commercial bank or REIT, which cannot issue tax-exempt debt.

IRBs, which were a mainstay of local economic development financing until the mid-1980s, have been much restricted in scope. Prior to 1986 they could be used for a wide range of projects, including wholesaling and retailing as well as manufacturing. After 1986 their commercial uses were restricted to manufacturing. After December 31, 1989, they were eliminated as a source of manufacturing finance and restricted to a small range of activities such as sewage treatment. However, local governments may still use their tax-exempt borrowing powers to raise funds for such purposes as building a municipal industrial park, clearing land in a redevelopment area, and so on.

2. *Loan guarantees.* The development agency guarantees the lender that it will repay all or a major portion of the outstanding balance in the event that the firm defaults. The funds to cover such payments may come out of the agency's general budget, or they may come out of a fund built from premiums charged for the guarantee. Guarantees have two effects. Because the risk to the lender is much reduced, lenders may demand less equity. That is, they may be willing to lend a higher percentage of the total amount needed and thus increase the leverage ratio of the project.[5] Guarantees will also make lenders willing to lend to firms that they would not deem creditworthy in the absence of guarantees. In this regard guarantees offered by local or state agencies fill a role similar to that of Small Business Administration loans.

3. *Revolving loan funds.* The development agency or a subsidiary essentially becomes a small-scale banker. The revolving loan fund may be self-sustaining after it is initially capitalized, or it may receive periodic infusions of outside money so that it can lend either at below-market rates or under riskier conditions than would a conventional lender, such as a commercial bank.

4. *Second mortgages.* A mortgage is basically a long-term loan that is secured by a lien on the property. In the event of default, the lender may take the property and sell it to recover the remaining debt.[6] A second mortgage is subsidiary to the first mortgage. In the event of default, the claims of the first mortgage must be satisfied entirely before any payment can be made to the holder of the second mortgage. Second-mortgage lending is thus riskier than first-mortgage lending. In purely private transactions second mortgages generally carry higher interest rates and have shorter terms than first mortgages because of their greater risk. A second mortgage from a state or municipal agency can make a deal more attractive to an investor in several ways. First, the second mortgage may increase the leverage ratio. A conventional lender might be willing to lend no more than 70 percent on a project. If a public agency will lend an additional 20 percent on a second mortgage, the leverage ratio is tripled. It is also possible that the second mortgage will make an otherwise infeasible deal possible. The investor may not have enough cash to do the deal solely with the amount that can be

raised from conventional lenders. Finally, a second mortgage from a public source may lower the average interest rate of the loan. If the agency that does the second-mortgage lending borrows in tax-exempt markets, it can raise funds at lower cost than a private lender and thus can lend at a lower rate. Then, too, with a public agency there may also be some measure of subsidy. That is, the agency may not be entirely self-financing, but may obtain some of its funds from the municipality's or the state's general revenues.

5. *Interest rate reductions.* Development agencies may lend funds at below-market interest rates as a form of subsidy. Whether this is more or less effective than simply giving the discounted equivalent as an up-front subsidy is arguable.[7] Two practical points might be noted here. First, the loan locks the lender and the borrower into a long-term relationship and imposes long-term oversight responsibilities upon the lender. If the lender does not exercise some oversight over the years, it may have cause for regret later on. To lend large sums of money and then not exercise some oversight to see that the terms of the loan are being adhered to is foolish indeed. A related point is that the actual costs of lending are not always as predictable as neat-looking financial calculations indicate. Formulas in books on finance do not take into account the real world matters of fraud, chicanery, and incompetence. As the S&L crisis clearly demonstrates, these issues are not to be taken lightly. At this writing it appears that the S&L scandals may be followed by comparable, albeit smaller, shortfalls by other off-budget agencies. The point is that lending without sufficient oversight over the long term can expose the lender to larger risks than just the default of an honest investor who through bad luck or miscalculation cannot make a go of it.

A comment on IRBs might be instructive here by contrast. The record on IRBs has been very good, in the sense that there have been few, if any, defaults. In fact, when the writer was engaged in the issuance of IRBs in the late 1970s and raised the issue of what actually happened in the event of default, his agency's bond counsel was unable to answer the question. The reason was that despite having been involved in a large number of issues for many different development agencies, counsel had never witnessed a default. In the IRB process the issuing agency immediately distanced itself from the issue by assigning all of its rights to a trustee. The bonds were not an obligation of the issuing agency. Rather, they were guaranteed solely by the assets they were used to purchase and any other assets pledged by the firm.[8] The bonds were marketed to buyers, most often commercial banks, that had the sophistication to examine firms' financial statements, guarantees, and so on, and the motivation to do so because it was their own funds that were being lent. That situation exposed the development agency to virtually no risk and no oversight responsibility after the signing of the closing papers. The lending of the agency's own funds, or of public funds, is exactly the opposite situation.

6. *Direct writedowns.* Agencies may subsidize development by direct investment followed by sale or lease at below cost. The community industrial park in which sites are leased at below cost is an example of this. The cost to the municipality is clearly known.

7. *Property tax abatements.* Many local governments will offer property tax abatements on new investment within the municipality. Generally such abatements are partial rather than full and are time limited. In some cases the abatement continues at a constant rate for several years and then ends abruptly. In other cases the abatement declines in steps and thus fades out gradually. Abatements may be offered as a matter of policy to all new development in certain categories or may be offered only in selected cases. In some cases abatements may be offered informally. No program is written into law, but an informal agreement is reached between tax assessor and prospect. The effectiveness of abatements is open to question. Most of the academic literature on them does not show them to be very important in the calculations of firms. The community should be aware that any abatement shrinks the tax base and thus necessitates a higher tax rate to maintain the same level of service. Thus, at the same time the abatement makes the community more attractive to the beneficiary, it makes the community marginally less attractive to every other firm.

8. *Investment tax credits.* Many states offer investment credits against the state corporate income tax. Some percentage of new investment in the state, for example 2 percent or 5 percent, can be subtracted from the firm's corporate income tax liability. If it is a 5 percent credit, then on $1 million of eligible investment the firm must pay $50,000 less in state corporate income tax. Again, arrangements vary greatly from state to state. In some cases the credit is discretionary and the firm must apply for it. In other cases it may apply to all new investment in certain categories. Some states have provisions that permit the firm to carry the credit over into years in which it has income, for the credit is of no use if it applies in a year when the firm has a loss and thus has no state corporate income tax liability.

9. *Venture capital funds.* As noted in connection with the states, the term "venture capital" is not a precisely defined one. In general it refers to investments in start-ups where both risk and potential are high. Usually, though not necessarily, the venture capitalist acquires an equity interest in the firm so that there is the possibility of capital gains if the firm is successful. These capital gains, along with loan repayments and municipal or state funds, can be used to capitalize further investments. Private venture capitalists played a major role in building the microelectronics and the genetic engineering industries. Venture capital thus has a certain cachet. But it is not for every community. It is inherently risky and presumably requires an entrepreneurial climate that not every community possesses.

FEDERAL ASSISTANCE

As noted earlier, many of the major federal programs are either gone or greatly diminished. However, there are still some sources of federal funding remaining. Community development (CD) funds may be used for a very wide variety of purposes, including economic development. Permitted uses include infrastructure construction, site acquisition and improvement, and loans to businesses. Thus CD funds can be used for virtually all of the same purposes as UDAG or EDA funds. From the community perspective, however, there is a difference, in that UDAG or EDA funds are earmarked for economic development, whereas CD funds are not. If the UDAG grant the city spent to acquire land really was a windfall, in that the developer would have done the project without it, this was not a loss to the city, for without the project the city would not have gotten the funds. Comparable comments might be made for IRB financing. The city was delivering a subsidy to the investor, but the subsidy was someone else's money. CD funds are quite different. They are the city's by entitlement, and a dollar of CD funds spent on one purpose is a subtraction from the funding of some other purpose. It thus behooves the municipality and its development agency to make certain that the CD funds spent on economic development are not just windfalls. As noted earlier, making this determination is not always easy.

The EDA is a source of funds, but its budget is small. In the 1970s the agency was funded at about $0.5 billion. In fiscal 1989 its funding was under $200 million. If one takes into account the effects of inflation, the agency is now funded at about one-fifth what it was in its 1970s heyday. The most important funding category is public works and economic development under Title I of the Public Works and Economic Development Act of 1965. These grants will provide up to 50 percent funding (80 percent in cases of extreme distress) for public works such as roads, sewer lines, and drainage to support local economic development. Thus a municipality might use EDA funds to defray part of the cost of a community industrial park. The application process is time consuming. For example, the applicant must assemble a committee that prepares a community Overall Economic Development Plan into which the specific project plan fits. Given the limited supply of funds, getting an EDA grant is a very competitive process. In fact, the agency notes: "In the absence of extremely high levels of distress, EDA funding is unlikely."[9] The agency also notes that it tends to favor rural areas and that, specifically, it favors projects which relieve economic distress in such areas. In short, the economic developer should be fully cognizant of the long odds before committing the substantial amount of time required by the EDA process.

The Small Business Administration (SBA) has a number of programs that the community economic development agency may use. SBA loans in general are reserved for firms that have been rejected by conventional lenders. The SBA offers guarantees to banks to encourage them to make loans they would otherwise deem imprudent. The role of the development agency is one of guiding applicants to banks that make SBA loans, assisting with paperwork, and the like. In general there is no direct outlay of agency funds, but there may be substantial expenditures of time. The SBA will guarantee up to 90 percent of loans up to $155,000 and up to 85 percent of loans to $750,000. In general, interest rates may not exceed the prime rate by more than 2.75 percent. This is a very favorable rate for a firm whose financial structure is not sufficiently strong to obtain conventional credit. In addition to loan guarantees, SBA makes some direct loans to firms that are unable to secure SBA-guaranteed loans. Numerous limitations apply to eligibility for direct loans. SBA loans are restricted to relatively small firms. In manufacturing the maximum firm size is 500 to 1,000 workers, depending upon the industry. In wholesaling the firm may not have more than 100 employees. In services, retailing, construction, and agriculture size limits are expressed in terms of annual receipts rather than number of employees.

The SBA also supports the formation of Small Business Investment Corporations (SBICs). These are private ventures that must have a minimum of $1 million of privately raised capital. The SBA will then guarantee three dollars of debentures (bonds convertible into stock if the buyer so chooses) for every dollar of private capital. SBICs are generally organized on a for-profit basis and really constitute a form of venture capital organization. Like other venture capitalists they may make loans, take equity positions, or do both. A variation on the SBIC theme is the MESBIC. The term, which no longer has a legal meaning, signified Minority Enterprise Small Business Investment Corporation and is still in widespread use. More properly these are section 301(d) SBICs. Rather than being specifically for the financing of minority-owned businesses, 301(d) organizations are intended more generally for "disadvantaged" individuals. Rules for 301(d) corporations are generally similar to those for conventional SBICs. Given the private nature of an SBIC, a body of government cannot directly own and operate one. However, the economic developer might encourage the organization of one by individuals concerned with local economic growth. A nongovernmental economic development organization might consider the formation of an ordinary or 301(d) SBIC as part of its program.[10]

Another program that may be of interest to the economic developer is the Jobs Training Partnership Act (JTPA) sponsored by Senator Edward Kennedy and then Senator Dan Quayle, and often mentioned in the 1988 presidential campaign.[11] JTPA replaced the Comprehensive Employment and Training Act (CETA) in 1983. The Reagan administration's primary complaint about CETA was that few people moved from CETA-financed training or public employment to unsubsidized private-sector employment. The JTPA may be used by the local economic developer to assist or recruit firms, but it must be understood that the act is primarily a manpower training program, not an economic development program. The act essentially routes federal funds to the states, and each state uses the funds in the manner it sees fit—subject, of course, to federal guidelines. JTPA funds are used primarily for the training of disadvantaged workers. The criteria for determining "disadvantaged" status vary from state to state but are basically economic. Most trainees are unemployed persons, though in some cases members of the working poor may be enrolled.

The key decision-making unit in the JTPA structure is the Private Industry Council (PIC). The act requires that a majority of the PIC members and also its chairman be from the private sector. The PIC allocates the JTPA training funds. Most of the training is provided by public institutions such as community colleges. The training may be quite general—for example, training people to obtain general equivalency diplomas. It may also be quite specific, focusing upon particular industrial or commercial skills. The economic developer might use JTPA as a tool by seeking to arrange to train workers in skills needed by a local firm or a firm the community is seeking to recruit. The legislation states that JTPA funds cannot be used to encourage firm relocation. Thus the act might be more useful in training workers to meet the needs of an expanding local firm than of a new firm.

JTPA funding is substantial. In the 1989–90 program year, funding for all titles combined approached $3 billion. How useful JTPA is for the economic developer, however, is open to question. Very few respondents to the author's survey cited it as being useful. One reason for this is inevitable. That act, as most of us would agree it should do, seeks to target most of its funds to those who most need help. But many employers do not regard the most disadvantaged members of the labor force (and people who have dropped out of the labor force) as being a source of high-quality labor. Regardless of whether this perception is correct, it is wide-spread. The largest single piece of JTPA funding (about $1.7 billion) goes to Title II-A, Training Services for the Disadvantaged. A smaller piece, about $283 million, goes to Title III, Employment and Training Assistance for Dislocated Workers. Employers might view workers trained under this title in a somewhat more favorable light than those trained under other titles. The other major title is IIB, Summer Youth Employment and Training Program. This is not likely to be of much interest to the local economic developer, though it may well perform a highly useful function from a long-term national perspective.

NOTES

1. For a text written after the passage of the Tax Reform Act of 1986, see William Brueggeman and Leo D. Stone, *Real Estate Investment*, 8th ed., Richard D. Irwin, Homewood, Ill., 1989.

2. William N. Weirick, "REIT/REMIC Strategies to Replace Syndications in Public/Private Development," *Real Estate Review,* Spring 1989, p. 71.

3. William B. Brueggeman, John Eisenberg, and David M. Porter, "Low Interest Rate Foreign Currency Financing for Real Estate," *Real Estate Review,* Fall 1989, p. 23.

4. Depreciation or cost recovery applies to structures and depreciable improvements but not to the land itself.

5. Leverage multiplies the opportunity both for profit and for loss. Consider an investor who buys a $1 million property with $100,000 of his or her own funds and $900,000 in borrowed funds. If the market rises by 10 percent, the asset is now worth $1.1 million and the investor's equity has doubled. A 10 percent rise in the value of the asset has been leveraged into a 100 percent rate of return on investment. Conversely, if the market declines and the value of the asset falls by 10 percent, the investment now has a market value of $900,000. At this point the owner's equity is entirely gone. A 10 percent fall in the value of the asset has been leveraged into 100 percent destruction of owner's equity.

Leverage also permits an investor to increase the rate of return on investment by taking advantage of the difference between the cost of borrowing and the rate of return on the investment. Assume an investor purchases a $1 million facility with $200,000 of his or her own funds. The remaining $800,000 has been borrowed at 10 percent. The building yields a 12 percent rate of return. From this $120,000 (12 percent of $1 million) we subtract the $80,000 of debt service (10 percent of $800,000). The investor now realizes a $40,000 return on a $200,000 investment. This is a 20 percent rate of return. Had the investor purchased the building entirely with his or her funds, the rate of return would have been 12 percent ($120,000 on an investment of $1,000,000).

6. This is something of an oversimplification. In general, taxing jurisdictions such as the municipality or the school district have precedence if the property is in arrears on property taxes, as is generally the case.

7. "Discounted equivalent" is the present value of all of the differences between the subsidized interest payments and the payments that would have been made at market rates.

8. In addition to not being an obligation of local government, IRBs did not count as part of the municipality's debt for purposes of statutory debt limitation. This was another reason for their popularity with local governments. IRBs are discussed in more detail in the first edition of this book.

9. *Federal Register,* January 17, 1989, p. 1874.

10. Information on SBA programs can be obtained from the U.S. Small Business Administration, 1441 L Street NW, Washington, D.C. 20416.

11. Information on JTPA can be obtained from the Department of Labor in Washington. A directory of JTPA organizations is published by the National Association of Counties, 440 First St. NW, Washington, D.C. 20001.

12

Labor Market and Fiscal Impacts

In principle, a community should not start an economic development program without giving some thought to the effects that this program is likely to have upon the community. These should include direct effects upon the public treasury, financial effects upon individuals, and quality-of-life effects that may or may not be readily translated into dollar terms. This is saying no more than "look before you leap." Then, once the program is under way, impact analyses might be done from time to time when decisions have to be made. For example, if a project will not come into being without a subsidy, the net benefit of the project to the municipality and its residents should be estimated to decide whether the subsidy is warranted.

Although the above seems obvious, the fact is that many or perhaps most programs are started without such analyses and generally proceed without them for many years. Sometimes programs are started because it seems like a good idea. The fact that other communities have them is often a reason for starting. Few politicians would care to be belabored with questions like "Why don't we have an economic development program when every other county in the state does?" Sometimes programs are justified with a sort of biological metaphor to the effect of "If you're not growing, you're dying." In some cases one will observe communities pursuing economic development when the need for it is quite debatable. Recall the reply to the author's survey cited in Chapter 1. What follows on anticipating the fiscal and labor market effects of economic development programs describes what is sometimes done and what might be done, not what is usually done.

LABOR MARKET EFFECTS

A new plant should exert upward pressure on wages in the community by increasing the demand for labor. In fact, unless one postulates an infinitely elastic supply of labor (the perfect mobility of the classical competitive model), it is hard to argue that there will not be some elevating effect. Even if the plant lowers average wages through a job mix that commands lower wages than the existing job mix, it should still exert some upward pressure on the wages for most job categories.

How large the wage effects of new economic activity are will depend on a number of factors. These include the following:

- The size of the new plant's labor needs relative to the labor market
- The availability of labor from outside the municipality
- The capacity of the municipality and its environs to absorb inmigrants
- The match between the plant's labor needs and the characteristics of the area labor force
- Unemployment, underemployment, and labor-force participation rates in the area
- The size of the expected employment multiplier.

All other things being equal, the larger the new facility with respect to the area labor force, the larger the wage effect will be. Conversely, the greater the availability of labor from outside the area, the smaller the effect will be. The greater the ability of the municipality or its environs to absorb migrants, the smaller the wage effect will be, because new households will augment the labor force and relieve the upward pressure on wages. The greater the mismatch between the plant's labor needs and the skills and experience available on the local labor market, the more likely the plant is to hire from outside, and the smaller the general effect on the local labor market is likely to be. If the wages of specialized workers from outside the area are substantially higher than the average of local wages, the plant may raise the area average wage considerably without appreciably raising the wages of the original area residents. The comments by Thompson quoted in Chapter 1 are relevant here as well.

If the local labor market is soft originally (high unemployment, underemployment, or low labor-force participation rates), the wage-elevating effects are likely to be smaller than if the market is tight. The reader familiar with macroeconomics may note the resemblance to the reasoning behind the Phillips curve. Where excess capacity is great, increases in demand result primarily in increased output. As excess capacity falls, increases in demand begin having larger and larger price effects. If one substitutes "employment" for "output" and "wage" for "price," then one has produced a labor market analogy to the traditional Phillips curve. All other things being equal, the larger the multiplier, the larger the wage effect should be.

Summers et al. cite a number of studies indicating that in small communities, new manufacturing activity does raise real median family income.[1] The spread in percentage increases varies very widely. How much, if any, of this effect is to be accounted for on the basis of upward pressure on wages is not known. A new plant might raise median family income by providing jobs paying higher-than-average wages to new residents. This would raise average income levels but not benefit the original residents. In fact, by increasing the pressure on prices within the local economy, it might actually injure them. A new plant might raise median family income by increasing labor-force participation rates, thus increasing the average number of wage earners per family, in the absence of any visible elevating effect upon wages. In brief, it seems fairly clear that new industry does increase average or median income in small places, but the components of this increase are not clear. This writer suspects that studies designed to separate this effect into its components would show large effects from direct wage and labor-force participation rate factors and smaller effects from the elevation of wage levels for particular types of work. However, at present this must remain only a supposition.

Economic development is often advocated as a cure for local unemployment. The effects of new facilities on unemployment are thus of considerable interest. Both the availability of labor from outside the area and the ability of the area to absorb inmigrants will reduce the effect upon unemployment. The match between the skill needs of the new facility and the skills of the unemployed will also be a factor. Evidently, the better the match, the greater the effect will be. A new plant that increases the demand for nuclear-instrumentation technicians will have virtually no direct effect upon the unemployment rate among coal miners.

A series of studies cited by Summers et al. showed a range of 1.0 to 43.0 for the percentage of new-plant jobs filled by previously unemployed workers. They use the term "unemployed" in its literal meaning rather than in the formal sense.[2] Thus, some of the unemployed workers hired may have been outside the labor force. Therefore the measured decreases in unemployment would be even smaller. The large spread in the percentages cited should make one cautious about the efficacy of economic development as a cure for unemployment. Even greater caution is probably advisable in advocating economic development as a cure for welfare dependency.

A series of four studies cited by Summers et al. on the poverty status of workers hired by new plants showed a range of 18.6 to 49.1 for the percentage of newly hired workers who previously had been poor, and a range of 13.3 to 27.2 percent for those workers escaping poverty as a result of being hired. All studies were done in areas in which the initial incidence of poverty was high.

In regard to both of these series of studies, Summers et al. note: "As one would expect, the higher-skill higher-wage firms attract few unemployed or poor individuals who typically lack the qualifications necessary to compete for such jobs. Thus, even in areas with significant rates of unemployment and poverty, new plants may not alleviate these twin problems if the skill level of the surplus labor pool and the new labor demand are not closely matched."

For the economic developer, insight into the above effects may present something of a dilemma. Bringing in a prestigious corporate headquarters or research and development operation may bring the approbation of the citizenry who pay his salary but do little for the poor and the unemployed in his and adjacent communities. Bringing in a low-skill assembly operation may do a great deal more for the unemployed and the poor but considerably less for the economic developer's reputation among his future employers. Perhaps this takes us back to Chapter 8 and suggests the value of a public-relations effort that educates the public about the rationale behind the development program. It suggests again that the definition of "desirable" development may be quite different if labor market goals are primary than if tax relief goals are primary.

Plant Openings and Closings

One might casually assume that the effects of a plant closing are the mirror image of those of a plant opening. This may be true so far as some tax revenues are concerned, but it is unlikely to be true for the labor market consequences. People tend to be much more mobile in the face of job opportunities than of job losses. Thus much of the employment effect of a new facility is likely to be soaked up by inmigrants. On the other hand, not much of the effect of job losses will be counterbalanced by outmigration of the newly unemployed. Thus a new plant of a given size is likely to have less of a lowering effect on the unemployment rate than the loss of an equivalent will have on elevating the unemployment rate. This brings us back to a point made earlier in the book. The first concern of most economic developers should not be the attraction of new industry but the nurturing of the community's existing economic base.

Multiplier Effects

Beyond the direct employment effects of a new facility there are likely to be some multiplier effects. New activity increases the demand for business services, raw materials, intermediate goods, and the like. The increase in wages and profits stimulates demand for consumer goods and personal services. A multiplier of 1.0 would mean that on a net basis the new project created no new jobs outside itself. A multiplier of 2.0 would suggest that the new project created one new job in the remainder of the economy for each of its jobs.

Though a good deal is known about multipliers for large areas such as metropolitan areas, relatively little is known about multipliers in smaller places.[3] However, some generalizations can be made.

1. The larger the place, all other things being equal, the larger the multiplier will be. This is because the bigger place will tend to capture more of the spillover. A large community will have more stores, more service businesses, more houses and apartments, and so on to capture the expenditures and incomes generated by a new facility. Physical size of the place is also a factor. If the plant is twenty miles from the nearest boundary, then more of its wage bill is likely to be spent within the community than if it is one mile from the nearest boundary.

2. The tighter the degree of linkage between the new firm and existing firms, the greater the multiplier will be because the new firm will purchase more of its inputs locally.

3. The higher the wages paid, the higher the multiplier will be. Though multiplier calculations are usually done in terms of workers, the key element is dollars. One stockbroker will generate more local employment than one file clerk.

4. The less overcapacity there is in the local sector when a new facility opens, the greater the multiplier will be. Before local businesses will hire more, the increased demand from the new facility will simply soak up the existing concealed unemployment.

5. The fewer supply-side limitations there are in the local sector, the bigger the multiplier will be. If local firms are able to meet new demands, there will be a greater employment increase than if the new firm must go outside the community for inputs.

Those studies done on small communities generally show small multipliers. Summers et al. summarize a group of studies that show a multiplier range from 1.0 to 1.71 with relatively few over 1.5. For five communities studied by Garrison, the figures are even lower, an average of only 1.08.[4] One reason Garrison suggests for these very low numbers is that much of the potential multiplier was soaked up by slack in the local economy—store clerks who spent much of their time waiting for customers to walk in, for instance.

For small communities that are not part of a metropolitan area, one might assume a multiplier in the range of 1.5. If the community is small and part of a metropolitan area, it is probably best to assume a multiplier of 1.0. So much of both the worker and firm buying power effect is likely to be exerted outside of the municipal bounds that it is best to assume no additional jobs will be created.

For a very large city or a metropolitan area it is hard to be definitive. Many studies done by urban economists have shown multipliers in the range of 3 to 4. These are done by dividing employment into an export (basic) and a local (nonbasic) sector. The multiplier is then calculated by dividing total employment by export employment. These studies may give misleadingly high results, however, because in recent years much of the local sector in many municipalities has been sustained by transfer payments to individuals and not through wages and profits generated in the export sector.

Can the multiplier ever be less than 1.0? If the new activity is local sector activity, the multiplier can indeed be less than 1.0, for the new facility may produce job losses in its competitors. For example, a new shopping center might employ 100 workers but cause a loss of 70 jobs among its competitors. In this case the multiplier would be 0.3. If the new shopping center were more efficient in that it sold more goods per salesperson, or if it relied more heavily on outside suppliers than did existing local firms, there might well be a net loss of jobs—a negative multiplier.

Housing Market Impacts

Housing market impacts are generally ignored, but they may be quite important. As noted in Chapter 1, economic development will almost inevitably increase the demand for housing. The elasticity of supply for the housing stock (how readily the stock can expand) will determine whether the effect manifests itself primarily in expanding the housing stock or primarily in driving up prices and rents. The size of the community and the amount of accessible housing in adjacent communities will also affect the amount that prices and rents are elevated. If the demand created by economic development in one community can be met by housing located in another community, the price effects may be minimal. If not, they will be larger. Among suburban communities the "we'll take the jobs, you get the housing" syndrome is very common. It is evidenced by the fact that land-use controls on housing are much more stringent. Rezonings from single family to office are far more readily given than rezonings from single family to, say, garden apartments.

Economic growth will also increase prices in general. Increases in the price of land, for example, are likely to be capitalized in rents and prices for commercial structures, which, in turn, will be reflected in the prices charged for goods and services. However, it is reasonable to believe that in most cases the other price effects will be substantially less than the housing price effects.

FISCAL IMPACT

The fiscal impact of economic development is the impact that is most often addressed. It is the easiest impact to calculate with at least the appearance of precision. Then, too, for the municipal government squeezed between rising costs and taxpayer militance, it may be of most immediate importance.

The goal of calculating the fiscal impact is to estimate how much surplus or deficit the proposed project will yield. One begins with the current level of both expenditures and taxes to do the calculations. If new revenues exceed new expenses, there is a fiscal surplus. This means that the current levels of service can be maintained at lower tax rates or that higher levels of service can be had at the existing tax rates. The reverse comments can be made if the calculations show a deficit.

Estimating fiscal impact is far from an exact science. Most studies use fairly rudimentary techniques and generally look at only part of the total effect. Most of the techniques in use have not been subject to extensive testing. To have confidence in a technique, one would have to know that it had been used a number of times and that retrospective studies had confirmed its accuracy. In general, this sort of validating evidence is scarce. It is difficult to measure the fiscal effects of a particular project in a community where new projects occur periodically. The ideal situation—one in which the community is in a steady state, a development occurs, and then the community lapses back into a new steady state—is rare.

Before discussing the state of the art in fiscal impact analysis, we might consider how economic growth might affect the fiscal situation of the municipality. Assume a single project, perhaps a new plant or an expansion of an existing facility. The facility itself appears on the municipal tax roll. In general, the contribution to the property tax can be fairly well anticipated. The assessor knows what is to be built and for how much comparable facilities are assessed. From that point on, however, uncertainty grows rapidly. It is reasonable to believe that there will be some multiplier effect attached to the new facility. How big this will be is likely to be a matter of some conjecture. This, the secondary effect on the commercial property tax base, cannot be foreseen with accuracy.

In general, economic growth promotes population growth. Population growth tends to promote the construction of new housing. That new housing will appear on the tax rolls. To gauge the size of this effect, we would have to know how many of the new employees will live in town. We would also have to know how many of these new residents will move into existing structures and how many will move into structures that are built to accommodate them. To think about this question, we will need some knowledge of the existing housing stock both in our community and in adjacent communities. We will also need to make some estimates about how many of the new workers will come from the town's present population. Some new workers will be people who were unemployed until the new facility opened. Some will be dual jobholders, people who have one job and take a second job at the new facility. About 5 percent of the U.S. work force holds more than one job, so this is not necessarily a trivial consideration. Finally, some of the new workers may be local residents who were not counted among the unemployed because they were not actively seeking work—the so-called discouraged workers.

The new population in town will contribute to the municipal coffers through sales taxes. After we have estimated their numbers, we will need to estimate their incomes and how much of their incomes they will spend in town on taxable goods and services.

Comparable uncertainties exist on the cost side of the municipal ledger. How much will the new residents cost in increased police and fire protection? How much will they demand in recreational and social services? And so on. If the municipality operates its own school system, a key question is how many school-age children the new residents will have.

A study that takes into account a full range of effects will necessarily involve a substantial amount of conjecture, though it may be, and should be, conjecture based upon solid evidence and not merely numbers pulled out of the air. A study that excludes many of the secondary effects will be less conjectural, but it runs the risk of ignoring important items.

The orthodox approach is to look at only direct effects; that is, to opt for controllability and precision at the expense of comprehensiveness. The writer's preference is to do the opposite, but that is clearly a matter of opinion and no more.

Burchell and Listokin, the best-known writers in the area, define fiscal impact as follows: "A projection of the *direct*, current, public costs and revenues associated with residential or nonresidential growth to the local jurisdiction(s) in which this growth is taking place"[5] (author's emphasis). They list six basic types of study and then note that of the six, four are appropriate to residential developments and two to commercial developments. The linkage between commercial and residential development is thus cut. But, this writer's reservations notwithstanding, the direct-effects-only study is the most common type.

Studying Direct Fiscal Effects

We turn now to studies of direct effects. Subsequently the chapter presents a casual but much more comprehensive approach. The first question to be settled when thinking about a fiscal impact study is whether to take a marginal or an average costing approach. This is true regardless of whether the project is commercial or residential. The average costing approach assumes that unit costs imposed by new workers or new residents or new structures are comparable with existing unit costs. The marginal approach looks at existing service delivery systems such as police and fire protection, and education to determine whether there is existing excess capacity. It then attempts to determine the new unit costs in the light of this capacity or lack thereof. The marginal approach is much more time consuming. It also will produce very different results for apparently comparable projects. If there appears to be some excess capacity in the fire department, the cost of protecting one more commercial development may appear to be negligible. But if that development absorbs all of the excess capacity, the costs of the next project, even if it is identical, may be higher by a large multiple because that project will push the municipality into new capital and personnel costs. For both of the above reasons, the average costing approach is much more commonly taken.

The two common approaches that Burchell and Listokin recommend for commercial projects are the *proportional valuation* and the *employment anticipation* models. Both of these models are very well described by Burchell and Listokin, so they will be given only the briefest description here. The practitioner interested in doing a study or in commissioning a study should obtain Burchell and Listokin's book.

The proportional valuation model is, in concept, an extremely simple average costing technique. All municipal costs are divided into a commercial and a noncommercial share. This assignment is made on the basis of assessed value, under the assumption that property value roughly represents costs imposed upon the municipality. The share of the total nonresidential expense assignable to the new facility is determined on a share basis. If the new facility will bear 2 percent of the total nonresidential assessment, then it is assumed to generate 2 percent of the nonresidential costs. Revenues are property taxes, real estate transfer taxes, and other taxes and fees paid by the facility.

The employment anticipation method is somewhat more complicated. It is a marginal approach that determines the increase in costs by multiplying the number of new employees by empirically derived factors for different categories of service in different size municipalities. The source of the multipliers is a table with headings such as "general government" and "public safety" across the top and municipal size classes down the side. Revenues are computed in the same manner as for the proportional valuation model.

As noted, neither model takes into account multiplier effects. Neither model explicitly takes into account residential effects, though it could be argued that the data used to develop the factors for the employment anticipation model do so implicitly.

A More Comprehensive Approach

This section presents an alternative approach embodied in a very simple computer model. The approach of the model is comprehensive in that secondary business and residential effects are included. One price of comprehensiveness is that the user of the model is required to guess at a number of questions. The quality of the results will depend, in large measure, on the accuracy of the guesses. There is no assertion here that this approach is better than the more orthodox approaches. It is simply presented as an alternative for the reader's consideration.

The programming steps can be read as if they were a series of instructions for doing the calculations by hand. The INPUT statements are steps that receive data and the words in quotation marks indicate what data is to be supplied. When reading the steps that do the calculations, be aware that in BASIC, multiplication is indicated by an asterisk. The words that appear to the right of apostrophes are not instructions to the machine, but notes to the user explaining what the step is doing. Steps beginning with REM (for reminder) also are not executed by the machine. They are more notes to the user. The steps that contain only a PRINT statement are for spacing and have no operating significance. The structure of the model is quite simple. In the first block the user inputs general data about the community; in the second block, data on revenues; and in the third block, data on expenditures; in the fourth block, project characteristics; and in the fifth block, some judgments about the future course of events. As soon as the user has responded to the last request from the machine (step 500), the computations are performed and the results appear on the screen. To use the program, type it into the PC. It will then be ready to use, though the reader might want to take another minute or two to save it on a disk. The REM statements, the empty "print" statements, and the remarks to the right of the apostrophes need not be typed in. To run the program, simply type the word RUN and push the "Enter" key. The question mark and legend from the first INPUT statement will then appear on the screen.

Although the model can be deciphered by the nonprogrammer, a brief account of its essential logic is provided here. Project employment multiplied by the user's estimate of the multiplier gives the total expected employment increase. This figure, adjusted for slack in the existing labor market, gives the total increase in new employees. The user's estimate of the percentage of new workers who will live in the community gives the increase in the number of new workers who will live in town. The user's estimate of the average number of new workers per household gives the number of new households. The new household figure, multiplied by the estimated number of persons per household, gives the population increase. The number of new households multiplied by the average number of schoolchildren per new household gives the increase in school enrollment. The calculations just described all rely upon estimates provided by the model user. The quality of results clearly depends upon how good these estimates are.

These estimates should not be pulled out of the air, but should be based upon something solid. For example, the number of workers in the average household might come from census data on the state, county, or municipal population. Average household size might also be based on census data.

The average number of schoolchildren per household might be based on the community's present experience. Total enrollment will be available from the school system, and the number of households can be estimated by updating the figures in the last census. The estimate of the percentage of new workers who will live in town might be based on data on the percentage of the town's work force that now lives in town. This percentage might be adjusted in the light of what is known about the cost and availability of land and housing in town as opposed to adjacent communities. The percentage of new retail sales that will be captured by merchants within the municipal boundary might be estimated by comparing the amount of retail floor space in the town with that in adjacent communities on the assumption that sales are roughly proportional to floor area.[6] In short, though precise estimates are not possible, reasonable estimates are readily made.

Property tax revenues from the project itself are based on square footage, assessed value, and tax rate numbers provided in the first block. Property tax revenues from secondary commercial development are assumed to be the same per worker as those from the project itself. Property tax revenues from new housing are obtained by multiplying the number of new households by the estimated assessed value of new housing and the tax rate. New sales tax receipts and new user charges and miscellaneous are estimated by assuming that new residents will pay these at the same rate as present residents. Thus, if population goes up by 10 percent, it is assumed that sales tax receipts will go up by 10 percent. State per capita aid, for both total population and pupils, is handled in a similar manner. The per capita figures provided by the user are multiplied by the computed increase in population and pupils.

The per capita approach is also used on the costing side with two exceptions. School costs are broken down into capital (debt service) and operating costs, and the user is asked whether new capital expenditures will be necessary. If the user says "no," only operating costs are adjusted. The model computes the present per-pupil operating costs and multiplies that figure by the estimated increase in enrollments. If the user says "yes," a comparable procedure is performed for capital costs. For utilities, it is assumed that 70 percent of costs are residential based and 30 percent are commercial based. Then it is assumed that in these two categories costs will rise in proportion to population increase and employment increase, as is appropriate.

The model is simple in both a conceptual and a programming sense. The same fundamental structure could be wrapped up in a much more elaborate program. For example, a correction loop could be added so that the user is shown the input data and given a chance to correct any value that has been entered incorrectly. Graphics subroutines could be added. The model could also be disaggregated further. Any one cost category could be disaggregated as far as the model builder would like. Utility costs, for example, could be disaggregated to the new-trash-cans-per-capita-per-year level if desired. Whether such disaggregation would produce better results is arguable. The big sources of error in the model are the judgment issues, and disaggregation does nothing to reduce that source of error.

The model has built into its structure some choices that are arguable. For example, school costs are broken down into capital costs and operating costs, but a comparable breakdown for recreational costs, social service costs, and such is not provided. The model could be readily modified to include such breakdowns. The model asks about slack in the labor markets. That is actually a marginal feature in an otherwise average costing model because if one project takes up the slack, then a second and equivalent project will show different labor market and, hence, different fiscal effects. That, too, is a choice. Additional sales tax receipts were estimated using the assumption that new households would have the same per capita income as households now in the community. But it would be equally valid to approach the question by starting with the estimated wage payments from the new facility. The model makes no allowance for jurisdictional overlaps. It would be appropriate for a county that constituted its own school district, but it would not be appropriate for a town within a county or even for a county in which education was provided by school districts that did not follow county lines. Given its simplicity, the model has some limitations that a larger model might not. For example, it has no internal checks for consistency or reasonableness. If the user tells it that the average household contains three people but sends five children to the public schools, the model will do the mathematics without pointing out that the data it was given are both unreasonable and logically impossible.

For the above reasons the model should not be seen as one that can be used off the shelf for a particular community. Rather, it is best regarded as a generic illustration of the sort of approach one might take to building a simple but relatively comprehensive model for a particular place.

The fact that the model is a computer model (albeit a very small and simple one) gives it no conceptual advantage over calculations done by hand. However, the computer model has a very large practical advantage in that it can be run many times. Each run takes only the several minutes required to enter the forty or so data items; the results appear instantaneously. One can thus do a worst-case scenario, a best-case scenario, a most likely scenario, and so on. It is also possible to do sensitivity analyses. That means that one can mathematically test the effects of changing one variable. For example, one data item the model asks for is the average size of new households. One might do one run with a household size of 2.8, another with a household size of 3.0, and so on to determine whether the cost/revenue ratio or the net revenue figure is sensitive to variations in household size. The capacity to explore different cases or scenarios is the big strength of the model. One cannot know the answers to any of the judgment items precisely. But by trying different sets of reasonable assumptions (and perhaps some extreme ones as well), one can bound the problem. If, for example, a series of trials shows a best-case revenue/cost ratio of 1.4 and a worst-case ratio of 0.9, one has quite possibly learned enough to make a judgment on the question at hand. One cannot say definitively whether the project will produce a revenue surplus or deficit, but one can say with some assurance that it will not be either a disaster or a great windfall. If a model is used not to pinpoint an answer but to bound the situation and get a range in which the answer probably lies, then it may produce useful results even if the data it uses are considerably less than perfect.

If the reader types in the programming steps in the model and runs it for a real community or for a made-up but more or less realistic data set, a particular fact will become apparent. The revenue/cost ratios will, in general, tend to cluster around 1. Results that are very far from 1 are hard to produce unless one makes extreme assumptions. Assuming the new plant will be assessed at $1,000 per square foot or that the average new household will send half a dozen children to the public schools will yield extreme results. Assuming that a modest-size community can add 1,000 new jobs and no new residents may, indeed, show a very high revenue/cost ratio. But unless one's assumptions strain credulity or the community is atypical in a major way, extreme results are hard to achieve.

This stability makes sense. If one takes a broad view of the community, it is apparent that economic growth often has the effect of scaling up the community. It increases both the tax base and municipal costs. If one thinks of the community's fiscal situation as being an equation with revenues equal to costs, then economic growth may, in effect, be like multiplying the equation by a constant. Both sides of the equation increase by the same amount. In the writer's view, the fiscal benefits of economic development are often oversold by its advocates.

A Run of the Model

The model was run with the data set shown below. We assume an industrial plant in a community that is fairly large physically, so that a substantial proportion of the new workers will live in town and a substantial share of new retail sales will occur in town.

Population	10,000
Public school enrollment	3,000
Property tax rate per $100	$2
Employment in town	3,000
Per capita income	$5,000

Revenues

Per capita aid (general)	$200
Per pupil aid	$600
Sales tax receipts	$500,000
Sales tax rate	2%
User charges, fines, and miscellaneous	$2,500,000

Expenditures

General administration and debt service	$500,000
Public safety	$1,500,000
Highway and traffic	$1,000,000
Utilities	$1,000,000
Parks and recreation	$500,000
Social services	$1,000,000
School debt service	$500,000
School operating expenses	$5,500,000

Project Characteristics

Employment	500
Square footage	250,000
Assessed value per square foot	$25
Annual sales	$20,000,000
Percent of sales subject to tax	25

Matters of Judgment

Size of multiplier	1.5
Absorbable slack in labor market	200
Percent of new workers who will live in town	70
Average number of new workers per household	1.5
Average size of new households	3.2
Average number of pupils per new household	0.6
Average assessed value of new housing	$40,000

The above numbers were entered in response to the prompting from the INPUT statements. In response to the final prompt it was indicated that no new school capital expenditures would be required. The results of the run were as follows:

Total revenue change	$831,358
Total expenditure change	$709,427
Revenue/cost ratio	1.17
New net revenue	$121,932

```
10 REM GENERIC AVERAGE COSTING MODEL
20 PRINT
30 PRINT
40 PRINT "This block inputs community data"
50 PRINT
60 INPUT "Population"; POP
70 INPUT "Public school enrollment"; PUPILS
80 INPUT "Property tax rate per $100"; PTAX
90 INPUT "Employment in municipality"; LOCEMP
100 INPUT "Per capita income"; PERCAP
110 PRINT
120 PRINT "Next block inputs current revenues"
130 PRINT
140 INPUT "Per capita intergovernmental aid"; PERCAPAID
150 INPUT "Per pupil intergovernmental aid"; PERPUPAID
160 INPUT "Sales taxes received"; STAX
170 INPUT "Sales tax rate as a percentage"; STAXRATE
180 INPUT "User charges, fees, fines and misc."; USER
190 PRINT
200 PRINT "Next block inputs current expenditures"
210 PRINT
220 INPUT "General administrative expense and debt service"; GENADMIN
230 INPUT "Public safety expense"; PUBSAFE
240 INPUT "Highway and traffic expense"; HIGHTRAF
250 INPUT "Utility expense"; UTIL
260 INPUT "Park and recreational expense"; PARK
270 INPUT "Social service expense"; SOCSERV
280 INPUT "School debt service"; SCHOOLDEBT
290 INPUT "School operating expense"; SCHOOLOP
300 PRINT
310 PRINT "PROJECT CHARACTERISTICS"
320 PRINT
330 INPUT "Employment in new facility"; DIRECTEMP
340 INPUT "Square footage of new facility"; SQFT
350 INPUT "Estimated assessed value per square foot"; AVAL
360 INPUT "Estimated annual sales"; ANNSALES
370 INPUT "Percent of output subject to sales tax"; PERCENTTX
380 PRINT
390 PRINT "MATTERS OF JUDGMENT"
400 PRINT
410 INPUT "Estimated size of multiplier"; MULT
420 INPUT "Absorbable slack in local labor market"; SLACK
430 INPUT "Percent of new workers who will live in town"; INTOWN
440 INPUT "Number of new workers per household"; WORKERSHH
450 INPUT "Average size of new households"; SIZEHH
460 INPUT "Average number of pupils per new household"; PUPHH
470 INPUT "Average assessed value of new housing units"; VALNEW
```

```
480 INPUT "Will new educational capital costs be incurred, yes or no"; A$
490 PRINT
500 PRINT
510 REM Steps below do calculations
520 PRINT
530 PRINT
540 EMPINC=MULT*DIRECTEMP                          'total increase in employment
550 NEWW=EMPINC-SLACK              'new workers regardless of where they live
560 NEWINTOWN = NEWW*(INTOWN/100)            'new workers living in town
570 NEWHU=NEWINTOWN/WORKERSHH                     'new housing units
580 NEWPUP=NEWHU*PUPHH                                'new pupils
590 NEWPOP=NEWHU*SIZEHH                         'increase in population
600 PRINT
610 REM NEXT STEPS DO NEW REVENUE CALCULATIONS
620 PRINT
630 PROJPTAX =SQFT*AVAL*PTAX/100      'new property taxes from project itself
640 SECPTAX=PROJPTAX*(MULT-1)/100    'property tax from secondary commercial
650 RESPTAX = NEWHU*VALNEW/100            'property tax from new housing
660 NEWPTAX= PROJPTAX+SECPTAX+RESPTAX         'total new property taxes
670 TAXRATIO = STAX/(POP*PERCAP)    'ratio of sales taxes to personal income
680 NEWSTAX=TAXRATIO*NEWPOP*PERCAP       'new sales taxes for local sales
690 PROJSTAX= ANNSALES*PERCENTTX/100*STAXRATE/100 'new sales tax from projt
700 USERCH=USER*(NEWPOP/POP)                         'new user charges
710 NEWCAP=PERCAPAID*NEWPOP                          'new per capita aid
720 NEWEDAID=PERPUPAID*NEWPUP                     'new educational aid
730 TOTREV=NEWPTAX+NEWSTAX+USERCH+NEWCAP+NEWEDAID+PROJSTAX
740 PRINT
750 REM NEXT STEPS DO NEW COST CALCULATIONS
760 PRINT
770 GENEXP=GENADMIN*(NEWPOP/POP)                     'new general expenses
780 PUBEXP=PUBSAFE*(NEWPOP/POP)               'new public safety expenses
790 UTEXP=UTIL*(.7*(NEWPOP/POP))+(.3*(EMPINC/LOCEMP)) 'new utility expenses
800 PARKEXP=PARK*(NEWPOP/POP)          'new park and recreation expenses
810 TRAF=HIGHTRAF*(NEWPOP/POP)          'new highway and traffic expenses
820 SOCEXP=SOCSERV*(NEWPOP/POP)            'new social services expenses
830 EDUCOP =SCHOOLOP*(NEWPUP/PUPILS)
840 IF A$="yes" THEN EDUKAP=SCHOOLDEBT*(NEWPUP/PUPILS)
850 TOTEXP=GENEXP+PUBEXP+UTEXP+PARKEXP+SOCEXP+EDUCOP+EDUKAP+TRAF
860 PRINT
870 PRINT
880 REM RESULTS
890 PRINT
900 PRINT "Total Revenues Change", TOTREV
910 PRINT "Total expense change", TOTEXP
920 PRINT "Revenue cost ratio", TOTREV/TOTEXP
930 PRINT "New Revenue", TOTREV-TOTEXP
940 END
```

More Sophisticated Models

Models which are far more powerful than the techniques described in Burchell and Listokin's book or than the author's "generic" model are available.[7] One example of a more sophisticated approach is the Virginia Impact Projector (VIP) built by Professor Thomas Johnson of Virginia Polytechnic Institute and State University.[8] The model was developed by cross-sectional analysis of data from many municipalities in Virginia. Because the model was developed from data from municipalities of varied size, it is able to do something which the traditional average costing model cannot do. Rather than using average costs of service (for example, so many dollars per pupil) it is able to relate the unit cost to the size of the operation. Many services provided by government have a U-shaped cost curve. As the scale of operation gets larger, economies of scale are achieved and unit costs fall. But past some point diseconomies of scale appear and unit costs begin to rise. For example, in a school system the diseconomies of scale might come from the need for additional layers of administration after some optimum size has been reached. The reader familiar with microeconomics will recognize the term "diseconomies of scale" as a synonym for "the law of diminishing returns," which presumably applies to all enterprises past some size. The model incorporates such non-linear cost functions.

The model, because it was developed from analysis of municipal expenditures, implicitly takes into account quality of service changes which may result from community growth. As a community grows its residents may demand a different level of service. Thus some of the change in expenditures results from changes in the level of service and not just from the necessity of providing the same service to more residents.

The model estimates some of the factors which the author's "generic" model asks the user to supply. For example, the VIP model estimates in-commuting on the basis of place size, population density, and other numbers which the user supplies.

The model has been used for estimating the fiscal effects of plant openings and plant closings and for estimating future costs and revenues under different growth scenarios. It has also been used in at least one lawsuit regarding annexation where the fiscal effects of a proposed annexation were an issue.

The model took several years to develop and test. When all of the faculty and graduate student labor used to build and calibrate it is considered, its total cost may have been as much as $200,000, clearly too much for most municipalities. However, when its cost is spread across many municipalities it becomes quite reasonable. The model operates on a spreadsheet that runs on a PC with an expanded memory. Though designed to be as friendly as possible, it is sufficiently complicated so that it takes several days of training to learn how to use it. Because of its much greater predictive power, this sort of sophisticated and comprehensive model may well be the wave of the future in fiscal impact analysis.

NOTES

1. Gene Summers et al., *The Invasion of Non-Metropolitan America by Industry: A Quarter Century of Experience*, Praeger, New York, 1976.

2. They use "unemployed" in the literal sense of not having a job. For statistical purposes people are defined as unemployed only if, in addition to not having a job, they are actively seeking work. When someone has ceased looking actively, they cease to be "unemployed" so far as the statistician is concerned.

3. The concept of the multiplier, a fundamental component of the export base model, is explained in any standard introductory work on urban economics. See, for example, James Heilbrun, *Urban Economics and Public Policy*, St. Martin's Press, New York, 3rd ed., 1987; or John M. Levy, *Urban and Metropolitan Economics*, McGraw-Hill, New York, 1985.

4. Charles Garrison, "The Impact of New Industry: An Application of the Economic Base Multiplier to Small Rural Areas," *Land Economics*, November 1972, pp. 327–337.

5. Robert W. Burchell, David Listokin, and William R. Dolphin, *The New Practitioner's Guide to Fiscal Impact Analysis*, Center for Urban Policy Research, Rutgers University, New Brunswick, N.J., 1985, p. 3. The reader might also wish to consult a more detailed work by Burchell and Listokin, *The Fiscal Impact Handbook: Estimating Local Costs and Revenues of Land Development*, Center for Urban Policy Research, Rutgers University, New Brunswick, N.J., 1978. For more details on costing out residential effects of economic development, consult George Sternlieb, *Housing Development and Municipal Costs*, Center for Urban Policy Research, Rutgers University, New Brunswick, N.J., 1973. The numbers will have changed. But the basic per capita approach is still equally valid. The figures on students per housing unit will have to be scaled back somewhat, since the data in the book reflect the higher birth rates of the 1950s and early 1960s.

6. For a rough estimate the model user might go one step further and take a gravity model approach. By analogy with gravitation, the force of "attraction" would be proportional to the amount of retail floor space divided by the square of the distance between the place of residence and that floor space. The concept of the gravity model, which was originally developed in the 1920s to model shopping behavior, and has since been greatly refined, is explained in many urban economics texts such as Levy, *Urban and Metropolitan Economics*, and in any transportation planning text, such as John W. Dickey, *Urban Transportation Planning*, McGraw-Hill, New York, various editions.

7. F. Larry Leistritz and Steven H. Murdock, *The Socioeconomic Impact of Resource Development: Methods for Assessment*, Westview Press, Boulder, Colo., 1981. Another bibliography with abstracts is *Fiscal Impact Analysis for State and Local Government*, Office of Policy Development and Research, Department of Housing and Urban Development, Washington, D.C., 1980. For further information on the development of econometric and input/output models for subnational economies,

consult Bureau of Economic Analysis, Department of Commerce, Washington, D.C.

8. Thomas G. Johnson, "Fiscal Impact Models for Virginia Communities," *Government Finance Review*, December 1988, pp. 36–38.

Local Economic Development in the National Picture

For the local economic developer the important question is how to play the game effectively under the existing rules. How the rules came to be the way they are and whether they make sense in terms of national objectives may be quite unimportant. For the reader whose interest is solely "practical," this chapter may readily be omitted. For the scholar and the student, however, the "big picture" discussed in this chapter should be of some interest.

A SHORT HISTORY OF LOCAL ECONOMIC DEVELOPMENT

Local economic development efforts are almost as old as the United States. In the early nineteenth century the merchants of many cities and towns organized to promote local economic growth. Such growth, then as now, was good for business and for property values. Modern goals such as relief of structural unemployment were absent. In fact, the concept that there was such a thing as an "unemployment rate," and that government ought to measure it, was absent. In the early nineteenth century, transport costs were a large multiple of what they are today. Thus the most effective step most municipalities could take to strengthen their competitive positions was to improve their access to the rest of the world. The great era of canal building in the United States, roughly 1800 to 1840, was largely the result of intermunicipal competition. The Erie Canal, completed in 1825, was planned and funded by New York merchants who correctly realized that water access to the Midwest would give the city an enormous advantage over its rivals, notably Boston and Philadelphia. Within a few years of its completion the canal was carrying close to a million tons of freight a year and New York surged ahead of its commercial rivals, in large measure because of the canal. It was, quite possibly, the most successful local economic development initiative in U.S. history.

About 1840 the age of canal building gave way to the age of railroad building. In many cases municipally backed bonds provided capital for railroad building. In other cases cities and towns bought railroad stock in order to provide capital. The competition to be on a railroad was intense. Writing about the now-defunct Oswego Midland Railroad, Eichner notes that it "zigzagged across the state in search of municipal bonds which were its principal source of capital. . . . Midland managed to cross the state for nearly 250 miles from Cornwall on the Hudson to Oswego on Lake Ontario without ever passing through a single major city."[1]

By the late 1880s the nation's railway grid was largely complete, and the focus of intermunicipal competition shifted to manufacturing. Subsidization to lure manufacturing became common. New England textile plants, for example, were brought to the South by capital supplied by municipalities and groups of local businessmen.

The first modern local economic development program is generally regarded as Mississippi's Balance Agriculture with Industry (BAWI) program, initiated during the Great Depression. The state authorized localities to issue tax-exempt bonds whose proceeds could be used to subsidize the building of industrial facilities. The state supported these local efforts with a promotional campaign to make Mississippi and its plentiful supply of low-cost labor better known. The emphases on promotion, low-cost financing, and state/local cooperation are hallmarks of local economic development efforts to the present time.

With the coming of World War II the Great Depression disappeared and the U.S. unemployment rate dipped to under 3 percent. The problem was no longer one of creating jobs but of finding workers. After the war the country entered into a long period of prosperity, and for a time there was little national interest in problems of local unemployment, though localities still pursued economic growth for reasons noted earlier. However, in time it was noted that in some areas of the country and among some segments of the population, poverty persisted regardless of how prosperous the country was in general. The term "structural unemployment" came into use and, beginning in the 1960s, the federal government began to fund both place-related and person-related programs.

THE FEDERAL PRESENCE IN LOCAL ECONOMIC DEVELOPMENT

Place-related programs seek to attack the problem of individual poverty by facilitating the development of places. This may be done by making the place a more desirable economic location, for example, by improving access or by lowering the cost of capital with grants, low-cost loans, and the like. The presumption that individual poverty can be ameliorated by place-related programs is based on the assumption that labor is not completely mobile. If labor were completely mobile, then job losses would produce outmigration of labor, and wage rates and unemployment rates would remain unchanged. Comparable comments could be made regarding employment increase. However, if labor is slow to migrate, job losses may produce long-lasting increases in unemployment and decreases in wage levels. Conversely, employment gains may generate long-term increases in wage levels and decreases in unemployment rates. This, then, is one of the justifications of place-related programs. Another justification is that the movement of population under the pressure of unemployment imposes large costs upon those who move, sometimes on those left behind, and sometimes upon society in general. The massive migration of American blacks from the rural South to northern cities as result of the post-World War II mechanization of agriculture is a case in point. It can be argued that place-related programs may be justified because they reduce the necessity to migrate and, thus, the attendant human costs of such migration.

People-related programs are the other blade of the scissors. If individuals have disadvantages that keep them from participating in the labor market, then programs aimed specifically at them, rather than at geographic areas, make sense. For example, if technological change has been rapid, it is reasonable that there will be a jobs-skills mismatch. Workers with obsolete skills will be unemployed while jobs demanding new skills go begging. Programs to retrain workers thus may make sense. If individuals have disadvantages that render them unable to compete economically, then programs to eliminate those disadvantages, whether they be educational, psychological, medical, or other, may make sense.

The first national-scale place-related program was the Area Redevelopment Administration, begun in 1961. This program funded industrial parks and other local economic development efforts. It was replaced in 1965 by the Economic Development Administration (EDA), which exists to the present time.[2] The EDA funded local efforts such as industrial park development, with eligibility based primarily upon county-level unemployment and poverty figures. The mid-1960s also saw the formation of regional development organizations. The first of these, and the sole survivor at the present time, was the Appalachian Regional Commission (ARC), an organization that extends through thirteen states, from southwestern New York to northeastern Mississippi. The ARC invested in both local development projects and regional projects. The largest share of its funds were spent on highways to open up the rugged terrain of Appalachia and make it possible for the region to compete with the more accessible East and Midwest that border it.

The Urban Renewal program, created by the Housing Act of 1949, was originally intended as a housing program. But with the passage of time it acquired a strong economic development cast. In its later stages many municipalities did urban renewal projects that had much more to do with economic than with residential development. The program was terminated in 1973 and was replaced the following year with Community Development Block Grants. These grants, given to municipalities on a formula basis, can be used for economic development as well as other community purposes. In 1977 the Urban Development Action Grant (UDAG) program began. A competitive rather than an entitlement program, UDAG provided grants for land acquisition, site improvement, and infrastructure development that were used by hundreds of communities. Another major source of federal funding for local economic development was not really a program but simply a few lines in the Internal Revenue Service code that permitted tax exemption on the interest on Industrial Revenue Bonds (IRBs). By the mid-1980s the federal tax expenditure (revenue losses) on IRBs approached $3 billion a year.[3]

On the manpower side the federal government entered the field in 1962 with the Manpower Development and Training Act (MDTA). The major thrust of the act was to provide support for heads of households while they were retraining for new, higher-demand occupations. When the national unemployment rate subsequently dropped, the focus of MDTA efforts shifted to specific target groups in the population, such as unemployed and disadvantaged youths. MDTA remained the centerpiece of federal manpower policy until 1973, when it was supplanted by the Comprehensive Employment and Training Act (CETA). CETA provided funds for both training and public-sector employment. As time passed, it became more tightly targeted to disadvantaged segments of the population. CETA's Achilles heel was that relatively few of the people who passed through it, whether for training or for public-sector employment, ultimately found their way into unsubsidized private-sector employment. As might be imagined, the Reagan administration, with its strong private-sector tilt, was extremely hostile to CETA. In 1983 CETA was terminated and supplanted by the Jobs Training Partnership Act (JTPA discussed in Chapter 11).

THE FEDERAL RETREAT

The 1970s was the heyday of federal participation in the funding of both place- and people-related programs. CETA funding in 1980 was about $8 billion, compared with somewhat under $3 billion for JTPA in 1989. If adjustment is made for inflation, JTPA funding is less than one-fourth that of CETA. As noted earlier, UDAG is effectively ended and EDA is now funded, in real terms, at less than one-fourth of its 1970s level. Changes in the IRS code had, by the end of 1989, restricted the issuance of IRBs to a very small range of public purposes. This turnaround has a number of explanations, but the primary one is ideological. Reagan campaigned for office by running against the federal government—as an outsider who would cut the monster down to size. And he won in a landslide. The administration took an essentially Friedmanesque view of the proper role of government and the relative efficiency of private-sector versus public-sector economic activity, and proceeded to act on that vision.[4] Milton Friedman had long ago argued that government expenditures were essentially revenue driven, and that they would rise to consume any amount of funds available. Rather than seeking to cut expenditures first and then cut taxes accordingly, the correct strategy was to cut taxes first and then let the pressure of the ensuing deficit force expenditures down. Congress took the bait of the Reagan tax cuts, and the downward pressure on many domestic programs has been a more or less permanent feature of the federal fiscal scene ever since. The Gramm-Rudman bill, with its mandated across-the-board cuts, flowed directly from the Reagan-Friedman strategy.

JUDGING THE SUM OF THE GAME

Although the federal government has retreated from the local economic development scene, intermunicipal competition is still extremely strong and probably has intensified in recent years. The federal retreat does not diminish the local motivations that drive the game. Most of this volume has been about how to play the game under the existing rules. But for the remainder of this chapter we turn to the somewhat more theoretical question of whether the rules are wise—does the game in its totality accomplish useful purposes? For the locality, gaining jobs for its citizens, ratables for its tax base, or profits for its entrepreneurs and property owners is desirable. But if the total effect of all local economic development activity is merely to shuffle existing assets, and if one community's gains come only at the expense of another community, then the game has no use when viewed at the national level. In the economist's terms, it would be a zero-sum game. In fact, if one considered the transaction costs, it might be considered a negative-sum game. The question, then, is whether the totality of local economic development accomplishes any useful purpose in the aggregate.

We might define two criteria for judging the net effects of the game: efficiency and equity. If the net effect of local economic development activities is to promote economic efficiency, we would have shown that the game, taken in its entirety, may be worthwhile. Similarly, if we could show that the net result of all local economic development activity was to produce a more equitable (fairer) distribution of wealth and income in the United States, then we would have shown that the game may be worthwhile.

To make the claim that local economic development programs contribute to aggregate economic performance, we would have to establish either of the following propositions:

1. Economic development programs, on balance, cause resources to be used more efficiently than would otherwise be the case.

2. Economic development programs cause resources that are not now in use to be brought into use.

Let us turn first to the question of efficiency. The earliest reference to this issue in the academic literature of which the author is aware is an article by Moes. He argued that allowing communities to subsidize firms could contribute to higher GNP by increasing total employment. The argument might be summarized by saying that if there are unemployed workers whose productivity is less than the wage that they can or will accept, subsidies that make their employment possible expand the work force and contribute to growth of the GNP: "Un- and underemployment are the results of wage rigidities. If wages were completely flexible unemployment could not persist."[5]

To illustrate this argument, assume that a town has a substantial number of former workers who have been unemployed for a long time. The XYZ factory would locate there if it could pay these potential workers a maximum of $3.00 per hour, because it calculates that their marginal productivity will be $3.00 per hour. The minimum wage law, however, stipulates a figure of $3.35 per hour. The town subsidizes the firm to the extent of $.35 per hour of labor, and the formerly unemployed workers are put to work. Workers whose productivity per hour was formerly 0 are now employed in jobs where their productivity is $3.00 per hour. GNP is now higher by $3.00 multiplied by the number of hours worked. Rather than distorting markets, as subsidies are generally thought to do, Moes argues that they may improve markets:

Competition for industry by means of subsidies tends to correct existing "distortions" in the market rather than introduce new ones. It takes the place of wage competition that would occur if wages were completely flexible and which in that case would direct additional investments to those locations where they contribute most to the national product.

If Moes is correct, local economic development programs, or at least their subsidizing activities, can be justified on macroeconomic grounds. But is he correct? Moes was essentially saying that by providing for downward flexibility of wages (in this example, letting the firm pay below minimum wage with the town making up the difference), the work force could be expanded. His critics pointed out that Moes's essentially neoclassical or Pigovian (after the economist A. C. Pigou) argument flatly contradicts a main point of Keynesian economics: the argument that workers cannot restore full employment by accepting lower wages because by the act of accepting lower wages, they reduce aggregate demand.[6] At this point the argument runs aground on shoals of macroeconomic theory beyond the scope of this chapter.

Regardless of theoretical issues, however, a very simple empirical argument can be made against Moes's position. At this time his implicit assumption that only labor-surplus communities promote local economic development is simply not true (though it may have been close to the truth when he wrote). The reason is that there are many motivations for pursuing economic growth other than prolonged labor surplus. Wealthy communities as well as poor communities play the economic development game. What is true of communities is also true at the state level. Every state pursues economic growth. Connecticut, the wealthiest state, plays the game just as assiduously as Mississippi, the poorest state.

If it seems doubtful that local economic development programs in the aggregate expand the supply of labor, is it possible that they expand the supply of capital? It is widely held that the United States as a nation saves (and invests) too little. Often this is attributed to a pro-consumption bias in the U.S. tax structure. For example, interest earned is taxed. But interest paid on many items is deductible. Let us assume that we do, in fact, overconsume and underinvest. One can then argue that the net effect of all the subsidies to industry offered by competing jurisdictions is simply a general subsidy to capital formation. All the IRBs, investment tax credits, community investments in industrial parks, and the like help redress the balance between consumption and investment, and hence improve aggregate economic performance.

However, even if one accepts the above argument, it must be admitted that the same effect could be attained with much lower transaction costs simply by making appropriate changes in the IRS code. Further, it seems evident that uniform, across-the-board changes in the tax code would operate with greater marginal efficiency than would the more irregular and capricious pattern produced under the present system of interjurisdictional competition. We might then conclude that subsidization may make a contribution to GNP, but that it does so in a clearly suboptimal manner.

Even though we grant some credence to the capital expansion argument, we must note that it collides with what we might call the capital efficiency argument. A subsidy, in effect, distorts prices. It makes the cost of the subsidized activity cheaper to the firm than would normally be the case, for the community (or state or federal government) is picking up part of the cost. Because subsidization distorts costs, the firm may not locate in what is, in reality, the lowest-cost location. In effect, a subsidy is a payment to be inefficient. Thus at the same time that subsidies may increase the total amount of investment, they may also reduce the efficiency of each unit of investment. We are left with a somewhat ambiguous situation, for we do not know which effect outweighs the other.

Is there any way local economic development programs make an unambiguous contribution to economic efficiency? The writer would argue that there are two such ways, somewhat related to each other. One of the primary functions of local economic development agencies is the provision of information. For reasons noted earlier, the information problem confronting the firm about to make a location decision can be a very formidable one. The better the firm's information, the better its decision-making process is likely to be. One characteristic of the perfect market of the economist is perfect information. The net effect of the information function of local economic development agencies is to move the market for sites and structures in the direction of perfection. Presumably this makes an unambiguous contribution to the efficient location of business and industry.

The ombudsman function of the local economic development agency is somewhat similar. Most agencies make every effort to facilitate the relationship between government and business. To the extent that economic developers smooth out problems over permits, land-use controls, and the like, they accelerate the rate of capital formation. This, too, would appear to be an unambiguous contribution to national economic growth.

DOES LOCAL ECONOMIC DEVELOPMENT PROMOTE EQUITY?

Equity, or fairness, is not a term with a precise meaning. In scholarly literature it is often used as a synonym for equality. Those actions which move us toward greater equality are referred to as being equitable. Let us admit that this is a far from perfect definition, yet agree to use it in this discussion. If a program produces an increase in income equality, let us say that it produces equity gains. There is no question that reducing degrees of income inequality was one of the motivations behind federal programs that support local economic development programs. For example, the Public Works and Economic Development Act of 1965, which created the Economic Development Administration, contained the following language:

The Congress declares that the maintenance of the national economy at a high level is vital to the best interests of the United States, but that some of our regions, counties and communities are suffering substantial and persistent unemployment and underemployment and that such unemployment and underemployment cause hardship to many individuals, and waste invaluable human resources; that to overcome this problem the Federal Government, in cooperation with the states, should help areas and regions . . . .

The primary criteria that the EDA has been directed by the Congress to use in determining eligibility for funding are poverty and unemployment. Municipal eligibility for UDAGs was determined by several statistical criteria, including poverty and unemployment. CDBG funds are allocated on the basis of a population-based formula that gives extra weight to the percentage of the population below the federal poverty line. Federal manpower programs from MDTA to the current JTPA all had or have rules and regulations designed to target the training and other benefits to poor and disadvantaged individuals and households. The federal view that local economic development programs are to be supported primarily to attack poverty is unmistakably clear.

Scholarly literature that has examined programs such as UDAG and CDBG has judged them largely on the basis of how well they targeted funds to poorer communities.[7] Thus the scholarly community has, in effect, accepted the federal view. For us to conclude that local economic development efforts, considered in the aggregate, achieve equity goals, we would have to accept both of the following conclusions:

1. Local economic development programs, on balance, have the net effect of shifting investment in the direction of poorer places.
2. Shifting investment in the direction of poorer places promotes a more equal distribution of income among individuals and households.

Another way of saying this is that we would first have to show that the net effect of local economic development efforts is to promote interplace equity, and then that interplace equity promotes interpersonal equity.

Let us consider the first proposition. Does local economic development activity reduce interplace differences? If only poorer places played the game, the answer would have to be "yes." Moes, in the argument discussed earlier, tacitly assumed this. But this is not the case at present. Most communities have some unemployment, and any community can use more ratables. Then, too, the business community will generally favor economic development because it is good for business. Finally, as noted, many communities pursue economic development because their neighbors do or because it seems like a good idea. The term "growing" has a nicer ring to it than "static," and certainly a much happier sound than "shrinking."

The question, then, is who plays the game better. It may well be that, on balance, poorer communities are more strongly motivated. After all, their needs are greater. On the other hand, prosperous communities have their advantages, too. They may, by virtue of their prosperity, have more resources to put into economic development. Their sound fiscal health may give them higher bond ratings so that they can borrow more cheaply. The community that does not feel desperate may drive a harder bargain with developers and investors and get more for its subsidy dollar. In short, whether poor communities more often outcompete prosperous or whether the reverse is true is not an issue that can be resolved by a priori reasoning. It is an empirical question that, to the author's knowledge, has not been investigated. One author, however, does report studies which suggest that wealthier places, on balance, appear to get a bigger return per dollar invested in local economic development than do poor places.[8] This does not answer the question definitely, but it is somewhat suggestive.

One might ask if, on balance, the total pattern of subsidies does not favor poorer places. Here, too, the answer is not as clear-cut as one might want. Direct federal subsidies almost undoubtedly have some bias toward poorer places because of eligibility requirements or funding formulas. But, as noted, federal funds are only a small portion of the total monies spent on promoting local economies. The other side of the federal subsidy to local economic development, IRBs, is shrinking in importance, as noted earlier. However, in their heyday the tax expenditure for them approached $3 billion per year. Virtually any municipality could claim some unemployment or some need for tax revenues, and thus meet the very loose public purpose requirements for such issues. The evidence would seem to be that poorer municipalities made no greater use of IRBs than wealthy communities.[9]

At the state level the picture becomes, if anything, even more muddled. Some states, such as Massachusetts, make an effort to target economic development funds to lagging areas.[10] However, states also tend to view themselves as a whole and to see themselves in competition with other states or even other nations. If that is the view, then earmarking funds for lagging areas or ruling prosperous areas off limits for state funding will be counterproductive. States support local economic development efforts with direct expenditures—for example, road construction—grants, and tax expenditures. Only about one-third of the states currently prepare a tax expenditure budget, and those budgets do not show the spatial distribution of tax expenditures.[11] Thus, the spatial distribution of state economic development outlays is not known. In the writer's opinion, it would be surprising if it were strongly pro-poor.

The second necessary condition, that increasing interplace equity will increase interpersonal equity, is also a matter of some uncertainty. If one postulates a huge difference in incomes between two places—such as exists, say, between the United States and Mexico—it seems hard to deny that equalizing the differences between the places will equalize the differences of their combined populations. However, if the differences between places are relatively small—comparable, say, with the differences between the various U.S. states—then it is not self-evident that increasing interplace equity increases interpersonal equity. One study suggests that the regional income convergence that has been occurring in the United States for a number of decades does not appear to promote a decrease in income inequality among individuals.[12] That finding does not prove that income convergence at the city or county level would not promote convergence of individual income. However, it does raise doubts, because at the local level the effects of place convergence are even more likely to be diluted by cross-commuting and migration.

The lack of empirical verification accords with what reason and experience might tell us. It is easy to suggest why steps taken to promote the economic development of poorer places may not tend to promote interpersonal equity:

1. Subsidizing capital investment necessarily delivers most of its initial gains near the top of the income pyramid. Water poured on the top of a staircase wets each step on its way to the bottom. And it wets the higher steps first.
2. The mobility of labor tends to defeat the equity effects of any place-related program, as indicated by the quotation from Wilbur Thompson in Chapter 1. The work of Gene Summers, noted in Chapter 11, suggests that much of the direct gain from new employment is captured by residents who are already employed. This further suggests that the trickle-down process is a slow one.

If the above lines of argument are correct, it would suggest that from a national perspective the unambiguously useful aspects of local economic development programs are the informational and ombudsman functions. These improve the quality of the locational decision by providing information, and they accelerate economic development by reducing the friction between government and business. Whether economic development programs, on balance, promote income equality is not known with certainty but, if the above arguments are correct, it does not seem likely that they achieve much in that direction.

The above tentative conclusions can lead to quite different policy prescriptions. An essentially conservative, market-oriented prescription would be the following. The informational and ombudsman functions serve a useful national function. Therefore, nothing should be done to interfere with them or in any way prevent communities from competing with each other. The subsidies associated with local economic development do not clearly perform a useful national function and, in fact, may distort economic decision making. On that basis we should oppose the subsidization of local economic development. The federal government has been correct in backing out of the game, and state and local governments should be encouraged to do likewise.

The political liberal would be likely to place more emphasis on equity and less on aggregate efficiency. He or she might then contend that if local economic development efforts do not now produce unambiguous equity gains, the rules of the game should be changed. These rule changes might include tighter targeting and more funding for federal programs. These would be coupled with tax and regulatory changes to prevent states from assisting prosperous places. Finally, the liberal might suggest laws and regulations that would prevent the more prosperous localities from offering financial incentives. In short, the liberal might propose to render the end results of the game more equitable by tipping the playing field toward the less fortunate players.

OTHER EFFECTS

To close, we might make one final observation about intermunicipal competition. The fact of such competition tends to shift the priorities of, and the balance of power within, local governments. For example, if the businessmen and the planners are at odds about a development issue, the fact of economic competition tends to weaken the hand of planners and strengthen that of the businessmen. For the business community can, often in complete truth, make arguments of the "if we don't, somebody else will" variety.

At this writing the municipality in which the writer lives and works is embroiled in a controversy over the rebuilding and widening of a stretch of road on which there is now much commercial development and which holds the potential for still more development. The lineup of the players is entirely predictable. Most of the residents, citizens' groups, and the planners favor a design that emphasizes safety and aesthetics. Owners of businesses and of land with business potential favor a design that permits maximum traffic flow and complete freedom to make any turning movement at any point. When the issue came up at a public hearing, the chamber of commerce weighed in with a pro-business presentation whose bottom line was, in effect, "If we don't please the business community, they may choose to expand elsewhere and our tax base will shrink."

It becomes more difficult for the municipality to oppose commercial interests, either in the actual event or in the anticipation of events, because of the recruitment efforts of other communities. Just as war or the anticipation of war strengthens the political hand of the military, so economic competition between communities tends to strengthen the hand of commercial interests as opposed to other interests. This is not necessarily bad, though the writer suspects that, more often than not, it leads to worse rather than better planning, but it is a fact of local political life that ought to be understood by the student of planning and local politics.

NOTES

1. Alfred Eichner, *State Development Agencies and Employment Expansion*, University of Michigan Press, Ann Arbor, 1970, p. 15.

2. CETA, UDAG, EDA, and IRBs are discussed in greater detail in the first edition of this book.

3. See Table 475, "Revenue Loss Estimates for Selected Tax Expenditures by Function, 1975–1987," *Statistical Abstract of the United States*, 108th ed., Bureau of the Census, U.S. Department of Commerce, Washington, D.C., 1987.

4. For a short, readable presentation of the ideological underpinnings of the economic conservatism to which the Reagan administration adhered, see Milton Friedman, *Freedom and Capitalism*, University of Chicago Press, Chicago, 1962.

5. John E. Moes, "The Subsidization of Industry by Local Communities in the South," *Southern Economic Journal*, 28, no. 2, October 1961, pp. 187–193.

6. Irving Goffman, "Local Subsidies for Industry: Comment," *Southern Economic Journal*, 29, no. 2, October 1962, pp. 112–114.

7. There is a large literature on this general subject. See, for example, Paul R. Dommel and Michael J. Rich, "The Rich Get Richer: The Attenuation of Targeting Effects of the Community Development Block Grant Program," *Urban Affairs Quarterly*, 22, no. 4, June 1987, pp. 552–579; John R. Gist and J. Carter Hill, "Political and Economic Influences in the Bureaucratic Allocation of Federal Funds: The Case of Urban Development Action Grants," *Journal of Urban Economics*, 16, no. 2, September 1984, pp. 158–172, and "The Economics of Choice in the Allocation of Federal Grants: An Empirical Test," *Public Choice*, 36, no. 1, January 1981, pp. 63–73; and Michael J. Rich, "Hitting the Target: The Distributional Impact of the Urban Development Action Grant Program," *Urban Affairs Quarterly*, 17, no. 3, March 1982, pp. 285–303.

8. Irene S. Rubin and Herbert J. Rubin, "Economic Development Incentives: The Poor (Cities) Pay More," *Urban Affairs Quarterly*, 23, no. 1, September 1987, pp. 15–36.

9. Thomas A. Pascarella and Richard D. Raymond, "Buying Bonds for Business: An Evaluation of the Industrial Revenue Bond Program," *Urban Affairs Quarterly*, 18, no. 1, September 1982, pp. 73–89.

10. R. Scott Fosler, ed., *The New Economic Role of the States*, Oxford University Press, New York, 1988.

11. Karen M. Benker, "Tax Expenditure Reporting: Closing the Loophole in State Budget Oversight," *National Tax Journal*, 39, no. 4, December 1986, pp. 403–417.

12. Mo Yin, S. Tam, and Joseph Persky, "Regional Convergence and National Inequality," *Review of Economics and Statistics*, February 1982, pp. 161–165.

Appendix: Economics for the Economic Developer

It is not necessary to be an economist to be a successful economic developer. Political acumen, ability to communicate with others—particularly bankers, businessmen, and politicians—a knowledge of finance, and a certain personal talent for seeing that one's own light is not hidden under bushel baskets are all more important for success in the field than is formal knowledge of economic theory. Nonetheless, some rudimentary economic concepts are useful, both in formulating the broad program outline and in explaining the program to citizens, businessmen, politicians, and others.

When questions of subsidization arise, it is useful to have a picture of the local economy in mind so that one can think effectively about whether it is worthwhile to expend public funds on the project. If subsidy funds are limited and one must choose between projects, it is important to have some concept of the functioning of the local economy so that one can make an informed choice.

Though what follows is taken from the field of urban economics, it is just as relevant to a small town as to a major metropolitan area. It is simple and inelegant but—this writer believes—useful and reasonably accurate. The picture of the local economy provided is the so-called export-base model.[1] A simple export-base model can be constructed from standard data sources in a few days. But even without building the model and doing any computations, the simple underlying concept of the model can be very useful in thinking about the local economy and about how events may affect it.

In looking at the economy of a place, whether small town, suburb, city, state, or region, one might begin by asking a simple question: From where does the money come? If we consider a city, we recognize immediately that the residents consume a great deal that they do not produce. In short, they import much of what they consume. How are these imports paid for?

In the most general sense, one must export to be able to import. Urban economists often divide the economy of a place into an export sector and a local sector. Sometimes the terms "basic" and "nonbasic" are used instead of "export" and "local."

What constitutes the export sector? Obviously, manufacturing is an export activity, with the exception of that share of the output which is sold locally. The same can be said for raw-materials extraction and agriculture. But export activity is not confined to physical products. A corporate headquarters that is sustained by corporate earnings outside the area is just as much an export activity as a factory. One might think of it as exporting decisions, studies, and administration rather than a physical product. Tourism, to the extent that it serves people from outside the area in question, is regarded as an export activity. Business services can be thought of as being part of the local or the export sector, depending upon which they serve. A law firm that devotes half its time to serving the needs of the resident population and half to serving the needs of firms engaged in export activity could be regarded as being divided evenly between local sector and export sector.

Retailing is generally regarded as a local-sector activity. But if a retailer sells partly to nonresidents, that part of his or her activity may be regarded as export sector. Thus, a neighborhood grocery store might be regarded as being entirely in the local sector, while a department store whose market area extends far beyond the community boundary is partly a local and partly an export-sector activity. Comparable statements can be made about personal services. The key question in determining whether an activity is a local or an export one is this: Where does the money that pays for the goods or services it provides originate?

In its most simple formulation, the export-base model consists of an export sector and a local sector of the economy. Local-sector activity is sustained by the money brought into the area by the export sector. When the flow of money into the area from exports is equal to the flow of money out of the area for imports, the area's economy is in equilibrium. If the flow of money in exceeds the flow out, the economy will expand. If the reverse is true, it will contract.[2]

A moment's reflection will suggest that this model grossly oversimplifies matters, in that many flows of money out of the area will not be for imports and many flows in will not be for exports. The pension that a retiree receives is not payment for an export, but it sustains the local sector of the economy, as do the earnings of a worker in an export industry. Similarly, the taxes a local resident pays to a higher level of government are not payments for an import, but they are still a subtraction from the money available to sustain the local economy.

Most types of payments are readily classified under the following scheme, which lists the various flows of money into and out of the local economy:

Outflows	Inflows
1. Payments for finished goods, semi-finished goods, raw materials, and services from vendors outside the area	Payments received for exports and for services rendered by area firms and individuals to parties outside the area
2. Taxes paid to jurisdictions other than the one in question, including both direct and indirect and personal and business taxes	Taxes paid to the jurisdiction by outside individuals and firms
3. Payments to parties outside the area, including rent, interest, royalties, transfers	Payments by outsiders to local firms and residents, including rent, interest, royalties, transfers
4. Expenditures made by area residents and firms outside the area	Expenditures made by outsiders within the area for goods and services

The payment a local manufacturer receives for a product sold to a wholesaler outside the area would be an inflow in category 1. Payments he or she makes to vendors outside the area for raw materials, components, or technical services would be an outflow in category 1. A pension check received by an area resident would be an inflow in category 3. An annuity premium by an area resident to an insurance company outside the area would be an outflow in the same category. Money spent in the area by a tourist would be an inflow in category 4. An expenditure made by a local resident while traveling outside the area would be an outflow in the same category. A new facility built in the area by an outside investor would entail a stream of expenditures classified as an inflow under category 4.

Obviously, many different but equally valid accounting schemes could be set up. In a closed system of communities, every inflow to one community would be an outflow to another. As in double-entry bookkeeping, the two totals would necessarily balance.

Returning to the idea of equilibrium, we noted before that when inflows exceed outflows, the level of activity within the system rises. The reverse is true when outflows exceed inflows. If the economic developer sees his or her function as that of increasing the total level of activity in the system, then this can be achieved in two general ways: increasing inflows or reducing outflows. Bringing in a new export industry will obviously increase inflows. Helping a local firm to begin manufacturing a product for local consumption that was formerly imported will reduce outflows. This is sometimes referred to as "import substitution." Helping a retailer build a facility at which purchases once made outside the area can now be made inside the area will also reduce outflows. But helping a retailer build a facility that will simply take away sales from other retailers within the area is playing a zero-sum game.

Urban economists speak of an export multiplier. Presumably, each dollar brought into the area by export activity circulates a certain number of times before it gradually leaks out. This concept is readily transformed into an employment multiplier in which each job in the export sector sustains a certain number of jobs in the local sector. Increases in export-sector employment thus cause larger changes in total employment. The ratio of change in total employment to change in export employment is the multiplier. If the local economy is such that there are very large leakages (perhaps most of what is consumed is not produced locally), the multiplier will be small. If there are fewer leakages, the multiplier will be larger. In a general way, large multipliers are associated with larger places because there is less leakage through imports. This point was discussed in Chapter 12.

For the economic developer trying to decide which of two projects is more deserving of subsidy, assuming that funds do not permit aiding both and that neither will happen without assistance, the key issue is likely to be which project appears to have a larger multiplier. In many cases the above ideas about inflow and outflow of funds should be sufficient to reason out the question.

Beyond the simple export-base model described above there are more sophisticated models. These include input/output models, econometric models, and various hybrid types. But their construction and use will generally require outside consulting services, and the question is whether the expenditure for this outside expertise is cost effective.

NOTES

1. For a description of the model, including information on how to construct one, see a standard urban economics text such as James Heilbrun, *Urban Economics and Public Policy*, St. Martin's Press, New York, 3rd ed., 1987; or John M. Levy, *Urban and Metropolitan Economics*, McGraw-Hill, New York, 1985.

2. The reader familiar with macroeconomics will note the similarity to the simple Keynesian model. In a two-sector model (firms and households), equilibrium is reached when outflows in the form of savings are equal to inflows in the form of investment. In the three-sector model (government is added), taxes appear as an additional outflow while government expenditures appear as an additional inflow. Again, equilibrium is reached when outflows are equal to inflows.

Bibliography

The following is a brief list of books and periodicals, most of which have been mentioned in the text. I am not aware of any significant work specifically on the public relations aspect of local economic development, and therefore have included two general works on the subject of public relations. For real estate financing I have listed the most recent textbook available so as to suggest a work that is adapted to the many changes brought about by the Tax Reform Act of 1986.

PERIODICALS

Area Development: Sites and Facility Planning. Halcyon Business Publications, Great Neck, N.Y.
Economic Development Review. American Economic Development Council, Chicago.
Economic Development Quarterly. Sage Publications, Newbury Park, Cal.
National Real Estate Investor. Communication Channels, Atlanta.
Plant Location, Boardman Publishing, New York.
Plants, Sites and Parks, Pocral, Coral Springs, Fla.
Real Estate Review. Warren, Gorham and Lamont, Boston.
Site Selection and Industrial Development. Conway Data, Atlanta.
Urban Land, Urban Land Institute, Washington, D.C.

BOOKS

Beyard, Michael D., et al. *Business and Industrial Park Development Handbook.* Urban Land Institute, Washington, D.C., 1988.

Brueggeman, William, and Leo D. Stone. *Real Estate Investment*, 8th ed. Richard D. Irwin, Homewood, Ill., 1989.

Burchell, Robert W., and David Listokin. *The Fiscal Impact Handbook: Estimating Local Costs and Revenues of Land Development*. Center for Urban Policy Research, Rutgers University, New Brunswick, N.J., 1978.

Burchell, Robert W., David Listokin, and William R. Dolphin. *The New Practitioner's Guide to Fiscal Impact Analysis*. Center for Urban Policy Research, Rutgers University, New Brunswick, N.J., 1985.

Cohen, Stephen S., and John Zysman. *Manufacturing Matters: The Myth of the Post-Industrial Economy*. Basic Books, New York, 1987.

Fosler, R. Scott, ed. *The New Economic Role of the States*. Oxford University Press, New York, 1988.

Haberman, David A. *Public Relations: The Necessary Art*. Iowa State University Press, Ames, 1988.

Malizia, Emil E. *Local Economic Development: A Guide to Practice*. Praeger, New York, 1985.

Moriarty, Barry M., and David J. Cowen, eds. *Industrial Location and Community Development*. University of North Carolina Press, Chapel Hill, 1980.

Quinlan, Joseph C. *Industrial Publicity*. Van Nostrand & Reinhold, New York, 1983.

Schmenner, Roger W. *Making Business Location Decisions*. Prentice-Hall, Englewood Cliffs, N.J., 1982.

Summers, Gene, et al. *The Invasion of Non-Metropolitan America by Industry: A Quarter Century of Experience*. Praeger, New York, 1976.

Index

About the Author

JOHN M. LEVY is an Associate Professor in the Urban Affairs and Planning program at Virginia Polytechnic Institute and State University, Blacksburg, Va. Before entering the academic world he was employed for a decade as a planner and economic developer. In addition to this volume he is the author of *Urban and Metropolitan Economics* (1985) and *Contemporary Urban Planning* (1988).

HT
123
L39
1990

Levy, John M.

Economic development
    programs for cities,
    counties, and
    towns.

$39.95

DATE			
JUN. 1 6 1992			